THE MYSTIC GRIMOIRE of MIGHTY SPELLS and RITUALS

Edited and re-published by

VcToria Gray,
daughter of Geof Gray-Cobb (aka Frater Malak)

The Alternative Universe
Edmonton, Alberta, Canada

The Mystic Grimoire
of Mighty Spells and Rituals

Copyright © 2019

Edited and re-published by VcToria Gray,
daughter of Frater Malak (aka Geof Gray-Cobb)

All rights reserved.
Printed in the United States of America.

ISBN: 978-0-9812138-5-9

First edition, 1976
Revised edition, April 2019

Published by The Alternative Universe
Edmonton, Alberta, Canada
www.alternativeuniverse.ca

This is dedicated to my late Father Geof Gray-Cobb, aka Frater Malak who left all his work to me. I have taken his book and re-published it. I have kept all the Spells, Rituals and Magic the same. I have removed all of the stories about how others received their Magic after using the Spells. This has allowed me to have a much smaller book and has allowed you to go straight to the preparation to allow the Magic to work without having to turn page after page.

The last chapter is mine. I have added one Spell for you all and a wee bit of information about my late Father.

If you need help with the work to be able to do the Spells or Rituals VcToria offers an option for you. You may order her help on her website store: www.alternativeuniverse.ca.

If you have purchased this book directly from the webstore at www.alternativeuniverse.ca you will find included "The Mystic Grimoire Talisman and Amulet Kit" which is impressed with the energy that the late Frater Malak used – and is necessary in order to work the Magic.

If you purchased this book from another online retailer you will have to purchase a Talisman Kit at www.alternativeuniverse.ca on the webstore. It is not included in the cost.

If you bought an e-book version the Kit is not included in the price and you will need to order it from the webstore at www.alternativeuniverse.ca.

You can also order more kits from the website if you require.

NOTE: This Grimoire is a magical tool. Any deliberate damage done to it, such as cutting pages, adding extra markings, writing marginal comments, underlining or interfering in any way with the contents will utterly cancel the effectiveness for you.

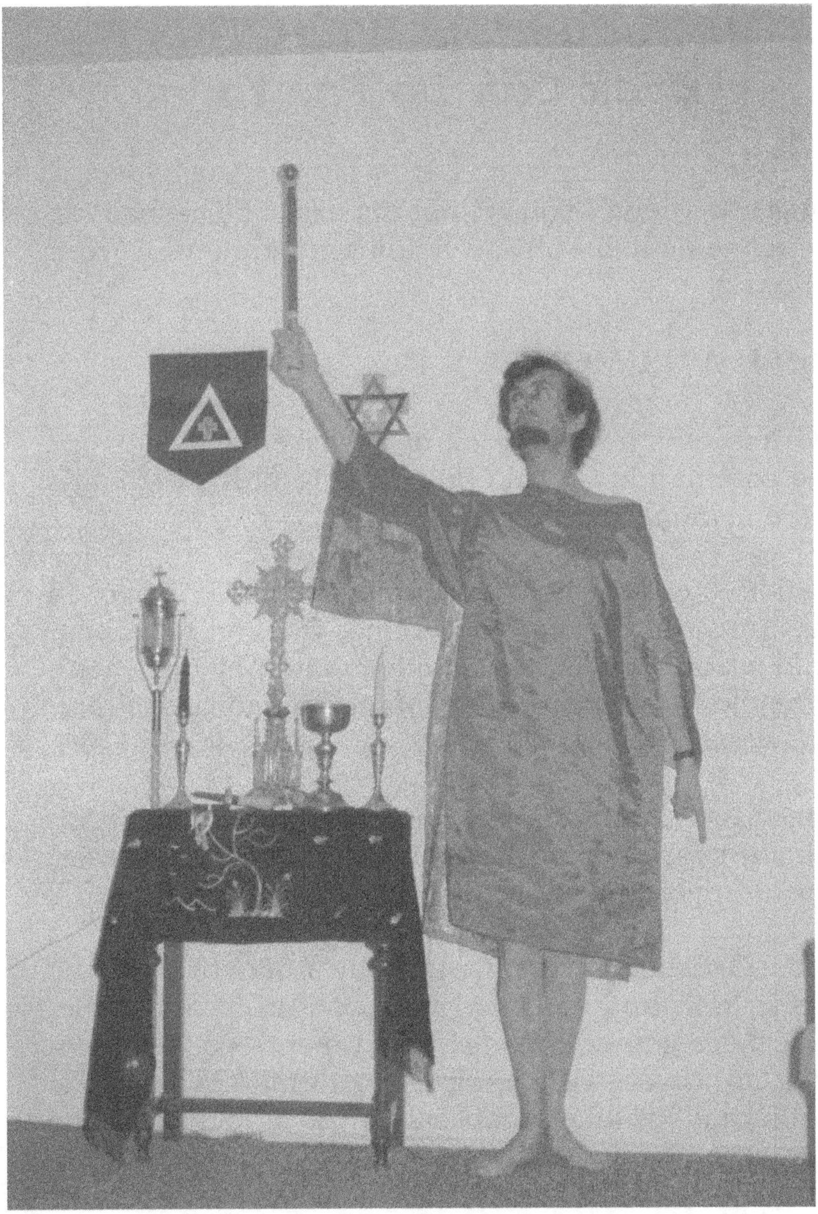

Geof Gray-Cobb (aka Frater Malak)

Introduction: What This Book Can Do For You

Congratulations—you've just opened a book that can change your life. You are holding a Grimoire in your hands.

What Is A GRIMOIRE?

A Grimoire is a hand book of a worker of Magic, one who commands Cosmic Beings to fulfil his demands in the mystic, unseen ways.

Grimoires exist which were written centuries ago. In museums and private collections, you can find these hand written books, personally created by dedicated, painstaking seekers after Magical knowledge and achievement.

Some took decades to put together, and each Grimoire varies in authenticity, accuracy and power, depending on the Magical status of the writer.

Some Grimoires were written by amateurs on the Mystic Path and are filled with confusion and fable. Others are genuine magical documents packed from cover to cover with explosive, ultimately powerful Spells and Rituals which can work Miracles for the user.

This is an authentic Grimoire. It is the ultimate condensation of arcane knowledge; knowledge accumulated in more than 35 years of research into the occult as I have worked my way up to become

INTRODUCTION: WHAT THIS BOOK CAN DO FOR YOU

one of the Regents of the Fraternal order whose teachings form a major part of this Grimoire.

Having condensed the data and selected the most superior Spells and Rituals, I have set them down in a logical, simple manner so that anyone can apply them to become, as I have, supremely rich, contented and powerful.

Swept aside are the confusions and disorder of the earlier Grimoires: you will find none of the false gewgaws of the fumbling beginner mystic, such as eye of the newt, wing of bat, graveyard dust, pacts with Satan and such futile and droll humbug. Here you have the bare bones of Magic, the true basic elements which work, efficiently and magnificently.

You can use them yourself. Follow the simple sequences of preparation and action, and you become the equal of any ancient Magic Worker who ever called on a Cosmic Being. And you shall see the identical results raining down on you in a veritable deluge of good fortune-money, health, love, power, fly to you irresistibly, as a needle is pulled to a magnet.

Pacts With The Devil? Not Here!

Before we go any further together, let me dispel a misconception.

The concept of the Devil is a relatively modern invention. When Magic was at its height, no one had even named His Satanic Majesty.

INTRODUCTION: WHAT THIS BOOK CAN DO FOR YOU

Yet over the centuries, a myth has grown up that in order to work Magic, you must use the Devil's powers or sign a pact with him.

You should pardon the expression, but poppycock! We're intent on doing ourselves some good, so naturally we call on benevolent Beings.

Let me assure you at the outset that every Cosmic Being named between these covers are good, obliging and has had His pedigree thoroughly checked out. Every Word of Power and every Angelic Name is associated with Holy and Blessed Writings from centuries in the dim and distant past.

Why Are Some People Lucky And Others Unlucky?

What is it which brings you good luck? What makes one person a millionaire, luxuriating among the good things in life, while many others wallow up to their ears in debt, in poverty and misery? Why is it that some people find a partner who fulfills their every desire, while so many others are sad and friendless, unable to harmonize with their fellows?

Coincidence Or Magic?

If you investigate the lives of successful people you'll find a coincidence operating: the coincidence of being born into a wealthy family; the coincidence of being in the right place at the right time; the coincidence of buying the right lottery ticket among thousands of losers...a thousand and one lucky happenings seem to surround the fortunate people of this earth.

INTRODUCTION: WHAT THIS BOOK CAN DO FOR YOU

But you'll also note that many successful people *stay* successful – not one lucky break comes their way, but hundreds of lucky breaks, until they are immersed in a golden stream of affluence and happiness.

One lucky break can be a coincidence. But a hundred lucky breaks? That's' kind of magical isn't it?

The Whole Secret Of Magic

Now listen: This book can bring you those lucky breaks, those exciting coincidences to change your life.

More than 20 years ago one of the world's greatest psychologists, Carl Gustav Jung, realized that things happen in this world which have no scientific explanations. His Theory of Synchronicity declares that Event A is always followed by Event B, *even though no connection seems to exist between the two events.*

Think about that for a moment, because that's the whole basis of this book – the whole Secret of Magic: ways of performing simple acts which produce results without scientific explanation, but which are designed to bring you whatever you need.

Miracles Are Yours

Yes, mighty forces around you *can* work miracles. Forces so powerful that man's greatest achievements and powers seem like trifles beside them. Forces which create earthquakes, raise mountains, make lightning, move the ocean tides, swing planets in orbit around flaming suns, and make the stars themselves flare with infinite energy. Energy which is part and parcel of this Universe.

You have the power to harness that awesome energy – to achieve exactly what you wish. The ultimate power is literally at your fingertips, to change your life into any shape you desire – easily, invisibly and automatically.

You Can Learn To Work Magic

Beyond the bounds of Science exists an area of creation which is but dimly understood by most people. Scientists admit, cautiously, that such an area may exist, but they have yet to pin it down, measure it and record its existence.

This area is the field of Magic, which you are about to explore.

Over the centuries, a few men and women have found the means to harness the Powers of Magic to bring ecstatic benefits to themselves.

You are about to learn their simple methods and join them.

What Do You Need To Make You Happy?

Just for a minute, let a parade of delicious thoughts run through your mind.

How would you like to have sacks full of $1000 bills? To develop ultra-potent sex appeal? To be glowing

INTRODUCTION: WHAT THIS BOOK CAN DO FOR YOU

with health and vitality? To have the world see you as handsome or beautiful, virile and intelligent? To be recognized as a power in your community? To win the lotteries, card games and other gambles whenever you please? To arouse any emotion you wish in another person? To know the innermost secrets of others? To travel invisibly into homes, offices and bedrooms to see and hear all that occurs? To banish bad luck forever and never again suffer a single frustration, setback or catastrophe?

Working Magic Is Easy

Yes, you can do all that, and more. The outdated idea that Magic can be worked only by talented people is false. Magic is for everyone – especially you. You have the ability to work the same miracles as the legendary Magicians of the past and the Secret Adepts of today, such as those in my Order, who work silently to achieve their desires.

Using Magic is as easy as learning to drive a car and is just as mechanical. The correct gestures, materials and words will work your Spells and Rituals – and every last thing you need to know is here in this book.

Your Personal Talisman And Amulet Kit

Inside the front cover of this book you will find one of the most powerful magical tools ever revealed by the Secret Lords of Flame, the Beings who permitted this book to be written for you.

The Mystic Grimoire Talisman and Amulet Kit contains 17 talismans and amulets which will form

INTRODUCTION: WHAT THIS BOOK CAN DO FOR YOU

an essential link between you and the Cosmic Energy Source which you will be contacting to work your personal miracles.

Secret Key III contains the simple instructions on how to use your Kit as part of your Rituals.

The sigils and symbols in the Kit are packed with occult energy. You will also find identical illustrations in the pages of this book – but note that they are only pictures: they do not have cosmic vibrations impregnated into them. It's the Kit which has the power: the pictures in this book are for your guidance only.

You will be instructed to cut the talismans and amulets from the Kit. Cutting them out of this book instead of from the Kit would be useless and counterproductive, because it would prevent the power of this Grimoire from assisting you.

Should you ever mislay your Talisman and Amulet Kit, or if your talismans need replacing,
The Alternative Universe website: www.alternativeuniverse.ca under the web store can supply you with a brand new replacement Kit for a nominal fee.

Try Magic, And See The Fantastic Results

I strongly advise you to read this book carefully through to the end before starting your Magic-working. Various supremely important instructions occur in the text which need to be observed if you wish to succeed. When you have read and absorbed the contents, you will be ready to start. Dipping in

INTRODUCTION: WHAT THIS BOOK CAN DO FOR YOU

and trying to extract bits of this Grimoire piecemeal is inadvisable if you're serious about wanting to transform your life.

Don't be in too much of a rush. All the instructions are here, simply expressed in a step-by-step order. Follow of them as directed, and you have the maximum chance of succeeding.

I shall mention this again later in the Grimoire, but please note that you must not mutilate, cut, mark, underline or make any additions or deletions to this book. Secret Key III explains why this is so.

I will not bore you with the tedious theory underlying this Magic. I ask only that you try it, and thus see its most important aspect – the startling, stunning results. Results which can bring riches, happiness and love flowing into your life. Results which can expel frustrations, oppositions, poverty and loneliness. You will make others cater to you, drive evil away from you, bring money cascading to you in glittering showers, win any lottery you wish, find glowing health, and transform a life of frustration into one of glorious ecstasy.

The Miracles Of Magic Defy Logic – Perform Them And Revel In The Results

As you travel this path of Magic you will be asked to do apparently illogical things. Remember at all times that scientific logic forms little part of the Miracles of Magic – in fact, Magic is beyond logic as science knows it, which is exactly why the actions, words and thoughts we use produce results which *seem* –

INTRODUCTION: WHAT THIS BOOK CAN DO FOR YOU

to the scientific observer – to bear little relation to the method.

But once you have performed a Spell or Ritual and seen the miraculous results, you will be above any criticism. You will *know* that a certain Spell or Ritual produces a certain result: you will have seen it happen to you, and no amount of scientific debunking from others who have yet to understand can affect your knowledge or belief.

And you will have the joy of knowing that if your critics should become too vocal or too pressing, you can vanquish them with a Spell or Ritual, leaving them gasping, hurt and puzzled, not knowing – because they tried to logically analyze the situation – exactly what hit them, or how they have suddenly been overcome and struck dumb.

You can be All Powerful. The Universe is yours to command. What do you want? In the pages of this book you will find out how to get it by Magical means. Read and wonder – but suspend your disbelief in these Miracles until they have worked for you. For that is all I ask: perform these Spells and Rituals, and you shall be happy, rich and victorious.

You Can Safely Modify These Spells And Rituals And Get The Same Perfect Results

As you learn to use the simple Rituals and Spells, you will be asked to do certain things, to use certain easily found items, to say certain Words of Power, at particular times and in particular places.

The Spells and Rituals are carefully detailed. All the

INTRODUCTION: WHAT THIS BOOK CAN DO FOR YOU

Secrets of Magic are revealed. Yet if a particular ingredient is unobtainable, or if you perform a Ritual at a time other than the one suggested, you will still see happy results.

The Spells and Rituals described are the ideal actions taken under ideal conditions. Many will work without every last detail being attended to – in fact, some will tell you that although maximum success will be achieved at a certain time, you can confidently perform the Spell or Ritual at any time, if the matter is an urgent one.

Perhaps you might compare a Spell or Ritual to an automobile. A complete Ritual, with all its details carefully performed, is like a finely-tuned car, with new tires, supercharged engine, overhauled brakes, rewired electrical system, free-flow exhausts and all the other extras which ensure it will get from point A to point B with maximum speed and efficiency.

Yet you know that a car will move without all of those refinements. Given gas, oil and water, almost any car will roll along the road reasonably well.

So it is with your Spells and Rituals. Apply all the suggested details, and you have the equivalent of a well-tuned car which will quickly and reliable take you where you want to go. Omit a few details of your Spell or Ritual, and it is like driving on partly-worn, but good tires, with a well-worn but still serviceable engine. You will still get to your destination, even if not quite so quickly and efficiently.

So a Spell or Ritual which is worked without every last detail included – for reasons of convenience or urgency – will still work for you. Be sure of that. But, whenever possible, attend to as many details as you can in a Ritual, and thus enhance your certainty of getting what you want as quickly and automatically as you wish.

The Forces You Use Are Benevolent, Not Devilish

The Forces you are harnessing have nothing to do with the evils of Satan. The Beings on whom you call for aid are benevolent and powerful: the old idea of "selling your soul to the Devil" in return for favors has no place in these pages.

The Powers you command are the very Forces of Creation. You will be using methods which have been learned by tedious experiment and time-consuming research from the Soul of Nature Herself. I know this research to be valid because it is used in my daily life as a member of our mystic Order.

Be happy, be strong and be powerful. I shall look for your name to appear in the headlines of the world's newspapers as you become steadily and miraculously more adept, more serene, more forceful, richer, happier and famous-all with the cooperation of these Cosmic Forces which work for your good.

Frater Malak

Revised very slightly by his daughter VcToria.
www.alternativeuniverse.ca

From the other side of the cosmos Frater Malak AKA Geof Gray Cobb, watches over his work that he left for the good of mankind. His energy, along with his daughter's, through her meditations, infuse the 17 talismans and amulets with the power needed to work the Magic of these spells.

Table of Contents

INTRODUCTION: WHAT THIS BOOK CAN DO FOR YOU viii

Secret Key I: Introduction 1

HOW THESE SPELLS AND RITUALS CAN AUTOMATICALLY BRING YOU YOUR EVERY DESIRE ... 2

    Apply The Science Of Magic And Be Supremely Happy, Rich And Successful 3

    Let Magic Bring You The Money Just As It Does For Me 4

    What Do You Wish To Change In Your Life? The Right Spell Or Ritual Is Here 5

    Tune In To Cosmic Power And Let It Bring Your Desires Into Glorious Reality 5

    The Difference Between Rituals And Spells 6

        Rituals 6

        Spells 7

    Which Are Best – Spells Or Rituals 8

    Be Unobtrusive With Your Magic 8

    Why Keep Magic-Working A Secret? 10

    Practice Makes Perfect 10

    When To Use A Spell In Place Of A Ritual 11

Secret Key II: Spells 13

TWENTY EIGHT RUNIC SPELLS TO MAGICALLY SMOOTH YOUR PATH THROUGH LIFE 14

    Spells Work Mysteriously 14

CONTENTS

Part 1: Four Superb Spells To Produce Wealth For You In Golden Torrents 16

    The Vital Bring-Me-Wealth Spell 16

    The Enterprising Ace-King Spell 17

    The Terrific Win-It-All Spell 18

    The Amazing Roulette-Certainty Spell 19

    Finding your Life Path Number 19

    Finding your Lucky Name Number 19

    Using your Numbers 20

    TABLE 1: Reigning Numbers of Each Hour of the Day 22

    Roulette Wheel Numbers Which Correspond to Your Lucky Name Number 24

Part 2: Three Lusty Spells To Give You Total Physical Satisfaction 26

    The Tantalizing New-Strength Spell 26

    The Occult Seduction Spell 27

    The Psychic Sex-Appeal Spell 27

Part 3: Three Vigorous Spells To Restore Your Health, Beauty And Potency. 29

    The Tremendous Beauty-Is-Mine Spell 29

    The Stupendous Young-Again Spell 30

    The Exciting Brilliance-For-Me Spell 31

Part 4: Four Dominating Spells To Give You Supreme Command Over Others 32

    The Haunting Horror-Producing Spell 32

    The Unseen Inner-Plane-Travel Spell 34

    The Crushing Disharmony-Exorcising Spell 35

CONTENTS

    The Staggering Return-Evil-To-Source Spell 36

Part 5: Three Personal Spells To Change Your Relationships For The Better 38

    The New Opposition-Begone Spell 38

    The Shattering Partnership-Disruption Spell 39

    The Mighty Attackers-Confusion Spell 41

Part 6: Five Practical Spells To Aid You In Your Job Or Business Dealings 43

    The Instant Business-Success Spell 43

    The Ancient Fame-And-Honors Spell 44

    The Fantastic Win-At-Law Spell 45

    The Glorious Move-Up-In-Life Spell 47

    The Wonderful Money-Aid Spell 49

Part 7: Six Exclusive Spells To Solve Your Life Problems 51

    The Startling Come-From-Above Spell 51

    The Expansive Bring-Me-Excitement Spell 53

    The Certain Danger-Stay-Away Spell 55

    The Brilliant Travel-Safely Spell 56

    The Protective Magic-Away Spell 56

    The Reliable Know-The-Unknown Spell 57

Secret Key III: Rituals 58

TWENTY SEVERN MASTERLY RITUAL TO MAGNIFICANETLY REMODEL YOUR TOTAL EXISTENCE 59

Part 1: Initial Preparations To Focus The Illustrious Cosmic Powers 62

CONTENTS

Rituals Change Your Life Effortlessly 62
Clearing Your Working Space 63
Clear An Area To Use For Your Magic 63
The Four Elemental Amulets On Your Altar 64
The Mystic Flame 70
The Thaumaturgic Triplet 70
Circle Of Protection 71
Expurgating Smoke 72
Your Magical Working Space Is Complete 72
Your Psychic Cloak 73
Psychic Cloak Power Induction 73
How To make Your Magical Oil 74
Your Mystic Talismans 75

Part 2: The Master Procedure Which Commands The Mystic Beings To Bring Your Goals Into Brilliant Reality 78

Modifying These Details Will Not Interrupt The Titanic Power Of Your Magic Working 79
Conditions For Assured Success In Magic Working 79
Working your Chosen Ritual Which Brings Your Personal Miracles Automatically 81
You're Working Your Magic, So Here Comes Happiness And Plenty 82
The Place-Cleaning Ritual 82
Continue Now Call Your Cosmic Beings – They Await Your Commands 86
Ending Your Ritual 87
The Dismissing Ritual 88

CONTENTS

Magic Working Is Simple And Automatic 88

Part 3: Four Enriching Rituals To Produce All The Money And Luxury You Can Imagine 90

The Rewarding Ticket-Come-To-Me Ritual 90

The Overwhelming Good-Luck-Is-Mine Ritual 91

The Great Money-Spinning Ritual 92

The Miraculous Gold-Creating Ritual 92

Part 4: Three Power-Packed Rituals To Satisfy Your Lust And Love 94

The Titillating Nature Ritual 94

The Irresistible Bring-A-Lover Ritual 94

The Stimulating Partner-Enslaving Ritual 95

Part 5: Three Miraculous Rituals To Restore Health And Bring Beauty And Potency To You. 97

The Supreme Back-To-Health Ritual 97

The Secret Disease-Banishing Ritual 98

The Fast Unwinding Ritual 98

Part 6: Three Crushing Rituals To Give You Supreme Power Over Others 100

The Explosive Eye-Glance Ritual 100

The Magical Win-In-Battle Ritual 101

The Volcanic You-Will-Submit Ritual 101

Part 7: Three Stupendous Rituals To Transform Your Personal Relationships 103

The Titanic Enemies-Vanquished Ritual 103

The Astounding Change-Opinions-Of-Others Ritual 103

The Power Take-Me-To-The-Top Ritual 104

CONTENTS

Part 8: Five Amazing Rituals For Success In Your Job, Career And Business... 106

    The Forceful Buy-Sell Ritual 106

    The Automatic Test-Success Ritual 106

    The Delightful Tell-Me-My-Powers Ritual 107

    The Thrilling I-Can-Wow-Them Ritual 108

    The Unique Know-What-Comes Ritual................. 109

Part 9: Six Ultimately Powerful Rituals To Bring Superlative Benefits To You. 110

    The Marvelous See-Where Ritual........................ 110

    The Ideal Change-My-Home Ritual...................... 110

    The Flashing Cause-Discord Ritual 111

    The Arcane Invisibility Ritual 112

    The Great Bad-Luck-Banishing Ritual.................. 113

    The Mysterious Enemy-Repulsion Ritual 114

Secret Key IV: Capitalizing On Rituals . 116

YOUR PERSONAL PROGRAM OF MAGIC-WORKING TO PRODUCE YOUR WONDERFUL HORN OF PLENTY ... 117

    Decide On The Miracle You Need First.................. 117

    Next, Dispose Of Minor Irritations Which Prevent You Enjoying Life To The Full 118

    When You Are Ready For It, Make Money By The Truckload 118

    Do What Thou Will, If It Harm None 119

Secret Key V: One Spell By VcToria 120

Secret Key I:
INTRODUCTION

How These Spells And Rituals Can Automatically Bring You Your Every Desire

You're going to work Magic with the help of this book. Real Magic – not the conjuring or sleight-of-hand of the stage magician. Magic working is simple and efficient, even if it has been described as superstition, delusion and fakery. Magic often generates fear, awe and envy. In fact, Magic is just about the most confused and misunderstood subject in the Universe.

But no matter what you believe about Magic, this book offers you a new approach – which works. And it clears away a great deal of the confusion and superstition which has surrounded Magic for centuries.

Long ago, longer than I'd like to recall, I decided that where the Miracles of Magic were concerned, a great deal of smoke was rolling down across the ages, hiding a very hot and bright fire at the source. I found I was right: although obscured by sensationalism, confusion and scientific doubts, true Magic will work for anyone. The right gestures and words, performed under the right conditions, will create miracles, no matter what the materialistic doubters insist.

Science, of course, has found many answers. Most of the luxuries and necessities of our daily lives are the fruits of dedicated scientific research.

SECRET KEY I: INTRODUCTION

Yet Science has so far used only a tiny part of this wonderful Universe. Along with the Natural Laws which have been discovered and used to shape our lives, powerful Cosmic Laws exist, and they are still awaiting full discovery.

You are here offered ways and means of applying those Cosmic Laws to your own life. These methods were at one time known and used by adepts to make their lives happy, harmonious and satisfying, and they are still being used in the Hermetic Orders throughout the world, such as the one I help to administer.

You have the opportunity – right now – to proceed a step beyond Natural Law. You can directly apply Cosmic Law, with proven methods which will show you their efficiency as they reshape your life to your own design.

Apply the Science Of Magic and Be Supremely Happy, Rich and Successful

Many centuries ago, men were more interested in results than they were in the theories. So the great Science of Magic grew up. Men were using the Law of Synchronicity long before Dr. Jung discovered it. They knew that certain vibrations – spoken words – and certain gestures, symbols and mixtures of ingredients would unfailingly cause miracles to happen. The combination of these vibrations, gestures and ingredients were called "Spells" or "Rituals".

Here, for the very first time in such simplified detail, you are offered the exact ways of changing your life

SECRET KEY I: INTRODUCTION

for the better, using the Science of Magic. Apply the straightforward recipes in the privacy of your own home – or even, unobtrusively, outside – and riches, happiness and success will flow towards you, automatically and inevitably.

Let Magic Bring You the Money Just As It Does For Me

The Spells and Rituals given here are easy to apply. *Why* they work remains a mystery which will be discovered later. I will not weigh you down with abstruse theories of how, for example, a certain combination of words and thoughts which I have called the Great Money-Spinning Ritual brings cash flowing to you.

I merely know that each morning I spend about two minutes performing that Ritual, and each day money comes to me, sufficient for my every need and more – sometimes only $20 or $30, sometimes $1000, occasionally $10,000. It all depends on how much I need to get through that day.

Anyone can use this Ritual. I know several dozen people who use it regularly and keep themselves in luxury. It is here for *you* to use, in Secret Key 111, and you can understand the joys of it. No more need you economize and try to save, putting money in the bank or under the mattress against future expenses. The worries of whether thieves will take your money, or the fears that the banks may go broke are removed from you all the time.

Just work at the Great Money-Spinning Ritual and enough money comes to you to settle your needs. Next day, work the Ritual again, and along comes

SECRET KEY I: INTRODUCTION

more money. The freedom and happiness this produces is indescribable.

What Do You Wish To Change In Your Life? The Right Spell Or Ritual Is Here

Transform your life into a new one of bliss and adventure. Cast off the restrictions of the daily grind, and let the ancient Cosmic Laws do your bidding. They only need prompting through the use of the Spells and Rituals offered here, and your life of frustration, opposition, fear and worry will be a thing of the past.

Somewhere in the pages of this book is a Spell or Ritual which will change any and all parts of your life into what you wish them to be. Try it – you're going to be surprised, delighted and blessed beyond your wildest dreams with health, wealth and happiness.

Tune In To Cosmic Power And Let It Bring Your Desires Into Glorious Reality

I promised I would not bore you with theories on why Magic works, yet you will want to know exactly what you are doing as you use the Energy of the Cosmos to turn your life into a stimulating, successful and joyous existence.

The instructions which follow in this book are all designed to do one thing: to tune your body and mind to centers of luck, power and influence which are just waiting for you to use them. It's very similar to tuning a radio or TV to receive a particular program, except that instead of turning knobs and

SECRET KEY I: INTRODUCTION

switches, you make certain Universal vibrations and patterns with your voice and body.

If you stand close to a piano, press down the sustaining pedal and sing or hum a note, you will find that after you stop, the piano goes on vibrating the note you have sung. You can actually hear that note. Try it sometime.

Or throw a pedal into a calm cool and watch the widening circle of ripples spread out until they reach the shore.

The whole Universe operates like that, and the words and gestures you are going to use in your Spells and Rituals vibrate the strings of the Cosmos, bringing your desires to reality. It's as simple as that.

The Difference Between Rituals and Spells

Magic is worked by the efficient techniques described in this book. Two basic methods are used: Rituals and Spells.

Rituals

Rituals consist of Magic working in a particular place, using gestures and words in specific patterns, at a certain time. The vibrations produced work with the energies of the Universe, and those energies shape your future into what you want it to be. Rituals work most efficiently when you choose the time and conditions carefully, prepare yourself beforehand and go through the techniques step by step.

Magical Rituals are ultimately powerful, and the

extra preparation needed amply repays you when you see the startling and fantastic results.

Notice that Rituals are not strange to you: we use ritual in our everyday life – physical ritual not magical ritual.

Driving a car is a type of physical ritual, with each action following the previous one, all aimed at producing a particular result.

You take the keys of the car, open the driver's door, put the correct key in the right slot, turn the key to the right, wait for the engine to fire, release the key, put the gear shift into drive, depress the gas pedal, release the brake, and away you go.

You could call that a car starting ritual. Leave out any step or try to do the steps in the wrong order, and you'd find that things were not working out right. For example, you must obviously climb into the car before you operate the starter, and if you release the brake before the correct time, you may find yourself rolling with a dead engine before you're ready to move.

Ritual Magic is little different. You go through a series of prescribed steps, and the results are achieved as easily and automatically as starting a car.

Spells

Spells use the same Forces of the Universe, but they rely more on thought patterns then Rituals do. Most Spells can be worked at anytime, anywhere, with

SECRET KEY I: INTRODUCTION

little preparation. Their advantage is that they are unobtrusive.

You can work a Spell among other people, where working a Ritual would attract undesirable attention.

However, if you are able to pick and choose your time and conditions of working, most Spells can be made stronger and more efficient, but you'll find as you progress and practice that many Spells have power to spare, so the results will come even if the time and place of working them was not precisely correct.

Which Are Best – Spells Or Rituals

Rituals are more powerful, but working a Spell is less noticeable to other people. Also, many conditions do not need the super high power Magic of a Ritual – a Spell is all the Magic you need.

Your major guideline is simple: if you have the time, are alone and no one can see you, use a Ritual. If people are present, use a Spell.

Be Unobtrusive With Your Magic

A very important occult maxim is: "Know, Will, Dare and Keep Silent"

The old Rosicrucian who coined that rule knew that the most successful Magic-workers are those who never breathe a word about what they're doing. You can be sure that if a friend of yours is forever saying: "I'm a witch" or often talks about the mystic power

SECRET KEY I: INTRODUCTION

he or she has, then that person is on a harmless ego trip.

True Magic-workers go about their business quietly, unobtrusively and secretly. No one – but no one – knows what they're doing, and when a Magic-worker achieves some success, he or she just smiles quietly and keeps silent. This is a basic credo in our Order, which is how we remain secret, successful and harmonious.

Follow that course of action yourself – it's very important. Magic itself works without fuss and without drawing attention to itself. Forget about the stories you have heard of bags of gold appearing out of nowhere, accompanied by peals of thunder. Disregard the tales of lightning bolts, clouds of green smoke, flashing-eyed demons and spirits, roaring voices out of space and similar spooky manifestations.

For Heaven's sakes, if you started those kinds of things going on around you, you'd soon have reporters and TV cameras making a nuisance of themselves, your friends and neighbours would run gibbering in fear, and you'd attract unwelcome interest from the authorities. You might even find the fire department trying to put you out!

No, Magic isn't like that. Magic works quietly behind the scenes to bring your miracles into reality. Occasionally you will see instantaneous, startling results occurring at once. More often, though, the Cosmic Machine rolls into action quietly and efficiently, and a little while later your wish comes true – *and it seems as if coincidence has caused it.*

SECRET KEY I: INTRODUCTION

Remember that. When your friends ask "How come you keep winning all those lotteries?" or "How come you've been promoted so quickly?" or "What's your secret for being so healthy and having such a harmonious love life?" or any of a hundred other envious questions, you do *not* say "I'm using Magic." No way: you merely smile, and say: "Coincidence, I guess."

Why Keep Magic-Working A Secret?

If you've read any books on Magic you'll know that the Magic-worker always instructs you to keep Rituals and Spells secret. The reason – as I've hinted before – is not because Magic is spooky, dangerous and awe-inspiring: it's because if you reveal that you've entered this marvelous area of existence, most people will react with fear or jealousy. It's that simple.

Sure, you can banish their fears and jealousies, or keep them at arm's length with a Spell or Ritual, but why go to that trouble if by keeping quiet you can be sure that the situation doesn't arise?

Go about your Magical business in secret, and let the Cosmic Forces work for you silently, efficiently and quietly.

Practice Makes Perfect

Magic depends for its operation on many apparently insignificant details – the phase of the Moon, for instance, is often a factor in success.

So you will sometimes find that a Spell or Ritual has

SECRET KEY I: INTRODUCTION

not worked as fully as you had expected. That merely means that one of the Universal conditions was not right at the time you performed it. So work it again, and again, if necessary. Sooner than you believe, you'll hit the right combination of time, place and Cosmic conditions.

And as you become more adept, you'll find that successes come quicker and are more satisfying: just like all other projects in life, practice improves your performance. Keep trying, and watch your successes multiply.

When To Use A Spell In Place Of A Ritual

I will repeat the rule I suggested earlier: use a Spell when other people are around, and use a Ritual when you have the time and privacy to prepare. A Ritual is long lasting, powerful and influential, while a Spell is quietly effective and sometimes works with a startling immediacy.

Personally, I reserve Rituals for long term important life projects and use Spells to smooth out the smaller problems of life.

The Secret Keys which follow contain 28 Spells and 27 Rituals. The Spells are carefully described in Secret Key II: what to do, how, and – if it's important – when.

Preparations for your Rituals, all of which are similar in their basic structure, are explained in detail in Secret Key III, while Parts 3 through 9 of that Secret Key gives you the details of each of these Rituals.

SECRET KEY I: INTRODUCTION

Feast your eyes on the banquet of Magic which is here set before you. Decide what you need, and let Magic bring it to you with quiet and glorious efficiency.

Secret Key II: SPELLS

Twenty Eight Runic Spells To Magically Smooth Your Path Through Life

These powerful, magical instructions are designed to allow you to achieve your desires without fuss and exhibitionism. If a Spell requires you to do something in private, it will say so, and when gestures or words form part of a Spell, remember to perform them without making yourself obvious to other people.

Also be reminded that until you become practised at the Art of Magic, a spell may require more than one application before it works to your entire satisfaction.

You need no special clothing or complicated preparations for Spells. Just carry out the simple instructions as given, and you will see that your most secret wishes come true with startling and joyful ease.

Spells Work Mysteriously

Great minds have puzzled over exactly why Spells and Rituals work as they do, and the only answer which has been reached is that although they undeniably *do* work with a mysterious efficiency, the reasons for this have yet to be discovered.

Yet there is no necessity for us to need to know those reasons, when we can gladly use the Magic to produce its exciting and satisfying automatic results. The proof of the pudding is in the eating – or,

SECRET KEY II: SPELLS

putting that old saying another way, the proof of Magic is in the glorious personal results!

SECRET KEY II: SPELLS

Part 1: Four Superb Spells to Produce Wealth for You in Golden Torrents

The Vital Bring-Me-Wealth Spell

This simple Spell has proven extremely successful for hundreds of users. It is concerned with bringing moderate amounts of money to settle existing debts.

As soon as possible after waking in the morning, write down on a piece of paper what bills need paying or what you want the money for. Keep it simple – write something like: "I need $1125 to pay the rent next month" or "I need $184.50 to bring my charge card payments up to date."

When you have written down your need, draw a line right around the statement. Keep that paper in your purse or pocket for at least 10 hours. Read it as often as you can during the day, *when you are alone and not observed.*

After darkness has fallen sit alone in a room and light a single candle. If you wish you can burn a stick of incense and have music playing. Put out all lights except the candle and read your piece of paper once more.

Then say:

> "Beyond this light the Powers come
> "To bring me this needed sum,
> "Aided by a Cosmic Name
> "Because I burn this Magic flame"

(If there is any likelihood that anyone would overhear you, just say the rhyme in your mind).

Repeat the rhyme until you have said it three times in all, then extinguish the candle. Tear your paper into tiny pieces and throw them away.

Repeat this Spell each evening for seven days or until the money comes, whichever is sooner.

The Enterprising Ace-King Spell

Poker? Blackjack? Bridge? Faro? You name it, and this Spell puts you out in front in card games where skill is needed.

Before you join the table, put your hands out of sight and cross the first two fingers of your right hand. Think the following rhyme:

> "High, low, black or red
> "Cards and luck to me are wed.
> "I know I'll pick up all the best
> "And stay ahead of all the rest."

Uncross your fingers, and come around to the *left side* of your chair as you sit down, and play the cards close to your chest.

Don't take stupid chances – play a normal game, let the Cosmic Powers do their work, and just watch things come your way.

SECRET KEY II: SPELLS

The Terrific Win-It-All Spell

This Spell needs a private place to set the luck vibrations going your way before you join a game or make a bet. It's designed to turn luck vibrations your way in contests where chance is the chief factor in winning.

Make sure you're alone and unseen by others.

If possible, perform this Spell during the day. Facing toward the sun, throw your hands and arms upward and outward, fingers straight and palms forward. Move your feet about 24 inches apart, so that you're standing in the shape of an X.

If it's after dark, face west if you are performing the spell before midnight and east after midnight.

Say, (or think if you maybe overheard):

> "Sun! Sun! The power that be,
> "The Gods of Chance shall smile on me,
> "While Lady Luck shall steal away
> "The fortune from my rival's play."

Lower your arms to your side, keep your eyes closed and touch your money, turning it over in your pocket or purse. Turn around three times to the right, stamp your right foot three times and open your eyes.

SECRET KEY II: SPELLS

The Amazing Roulette-Certainty Spell

You need to do a little work before you perform this Spell at the roulette table, but the results amply repay your trouble.

First, you need to know your Life Path Number and your Lucky Name Number.

Finding your Life Path Number

Write down your birth date in figures. If, for example, you were born on July 18, 1924, you would write 7. 18. 1924. Now add those numbers in a column.

In the above example you would add 7. Then add 1+8 = 9 and then 1+9+2+4=16. Because 16 is still not a single digit we add 1+6=7. Now add your three single digits 7+9+7=23. Now add those two digits and you get the number 5.

Whatever result you get, keep adding those numbers together until they are a single digit.

That final, single number is your Life Path Number. If zero comes anywhere in this simple calculation, just add it as such (i.e., 10 1+0=1).

Finding your Lucky Name Number

Sign your name just as you do on a cheque, contract or any paper that needs a signature. Leave out any titles as in Mr. Mrs. Ms. Just use your everyday name.

SECRET KEY II: SPELLS

Now give numbers to each of your letters of your name, using the following numerological value:

A=1 B=2 C=3 D=4 E=5 F=6 G=7 H=8 I=9 J=1 K=2 L=3 M=4 N=5 O=6 P=7 Q=8 R=9 S=1 T=2 U=3 V=4 W=5 X=6 Y=7 Z=8.

When you have done this, add the numbers together just as you did for the Life Path number. Each name part needs to be added to a singular digit then placed in a column and added to the next name part. Once you have all the numbers in a column add them up and with the answer. Keep adding that till it reaches a single digit number.

Example:

JOSEPH D. MALKIN
161578 4 413295

First: total =1+6+1+5+7+8 =28: 2+8 =10: 1+0 =1

Second: = 4

Third: = 4+1+3+2+9+5 =24: 2+4 =6

Take the 1+4+6 =11 and now 1+1 =2

Joseph D. Malkin has found his Lucky Name Number and it is a 2.

Using your Numbers

Find yourself a place at a roulette table, have a few chips ready and then check the time. That's

SECRET KEY II: SPELLS

important: you need to know what hour of the day you're gambling.

Take a look at Table 1. See below. It shows the reigning number of each hour of the day. That's the third number you use in applying the Amazing Roulette-Certainty spell.

Add together the Number of the Hour and your Life Path Number. Reduce it to a single digit if necessary. Call that number your Bet Number.

Now here's how and when to lay down your chips.

As soon as you've discovered your Bet Number, pay attention to the dealer. Sit back and watch the roll of the little ball. The spins of the wheel you're going to bet on are the ones which correspond to your Bet Number, and the actual numbers you're going to lay your chips on are those which total to your Lucky Name Number – and there are always four of those on a roulette wheel.

SECRET KEY II: SPELLS

TABLE 1: Reigning Numbers of Each Hour of the Day

Time	Number Of The Hour
Midnight to 12.59 a.m.	1
1.00 a.m. to 1.59 a.m.	2
2.00 a.m. to 2.59 a.m.	3
3.00 a.m. to 3.59 a.m.	4
4.00 a.m. to 4.59 a.m.	5
5.00 a.m. to 5.59 a.m.	6
6.00 a.m. to 6.59 a.m.	7
7.00 a.m. to 7.59 a.m.	8
8.00 a.m. to 8.59 a.m.	9
9.00 a.m. to 9.59 a.m.	1
10.00 a.m. to 10.59 a.m.	2
11.00 a.m. to 11.59 a.m.	3
Noon to 12.59 p.m.	4
1.00 p.m. to 1.59 p.m.	5
2.00 p.m. to 2.59 p.m.	6
3.00 p.m. to 3.59 p.m.	7
4.00 p.m. to 4.59 p.m.	8
5.00 p.m. to 5.59 p.m.	9
6.00 p.m. to 6.59 p.m.	1
7.00 p.m. to 7.59 p.m.	2
8.00 p.m. to 8.59 p.m.	3
9.00 p.m. to 9.59 p.m.	4
10.00 p.m. to 10.59 p.m.	5
11.00 p.m. to 11.59 p.m.	6

To make it crystal clear for you, Table 2 [see below] shows the numbers on the roulette wheel which correspond to the numbers 1 through 9.

SECRET KEY II: SPELLS

Here is the example you would use from the Life Path Number and Lucky Number

*Let's review the example of the Life Path Number and Lucky Name Number of Joe D. Malken. His Life Path Number was 5 and his Lucky Name Number was 2.

He sets himself down at the roulette table a few minutes after 8 P.M.

Take a look at table 1 again between 8 P.M. and 8:59 P.M. [these are local times by the way] and the number of the hour is three for Joe.

Now Joe totals his Life Path number 5 with the Hour Number 3. That equals 8.

Now Joe watches the spin of the wheel. He's going to lay down his chips at the *eighth* spin of the wheel – because his Bet Number is 8.

First spend; no bet. Second spin: no bet. And so on until the seventh spin is over.

On the eighth spin you lay the money. Joe's lucky name number is 2. There are four numbers on the wheel which correspond to 2: they are 2 [of course]; 11 [that's 1+1]; 20 [that's 2 add zero]; and lastly 29 [that's 2+9 = 11 which is a double figure so we add 1+1 and equals 2] got it?

Joe lays a single chip on 2, 11, 20 and 29. Then he sits back and lets the wheel spin. He stands to win 33 chips. But win or lose, Joe is now going to sit back and let the wheel spin another seven times

SECRET KEY II: SPELLS

without a bet. On the eighth spin he bets again on 2, 11, 20 and 29. And so it goes, keeping an eye on the clock, because at 9 P.M., the number of the hour becomes 4, which alters Joe's Bet Number. It does not, however, alter his Lucky Name Number or the numbers he lays his chips on.

Now that's not as complicated as it sounds. You're betting on the spins of the wheel spaced apart by your Bet Number, and your chips go down on your Lucky Name Numbers every time you bet.

Roulette Wheel Numbers Which Correspond to Your Lucky Name Number

Table 2:

Your Lucky Name Number	Corresponding Roulette Wheel Numbers To Bet On
1	1, 10, 19, 28
2	2, 11, 20, 29
3	3, 12, 21, 30
4	4, 13, 22, 31
5	5, 14, 23, 32
6	6, 15, 24, 33
7	7, 16, 25, 34
8	8, 17, 26, 35
9	9, 18, 27, 36

The first spin, the one you start counting from, starts as the dealer releases the ball for the first time after you've written down [or mentally calculated] your Bet Number.

SECRET KEY II: SPELLS

Every hour, on the hour, recalculate your new Bet Number. Then start counting the spins of the wheel for the new sequence, exactly as you did when you first started.

This automatic Spell puts you right into your luck patterns: if it's possible to win, you'll win big with that Spell. Give it a whirl – many other people have, and they've been amazed.

Caution

The Powers governing personal gambling luck are easily influenced, but notoriously fickle for that same reason.

It is possible for others involved in a game with you to be – deliberately or unknowingly – using a Spell or Ritual which at that time is more powerful than yours.

This will naturally affect, and possibly cancel, your own Magic. In that case – and you will recognize this by the fact that your early bets are losers – leave the casino at once and return at some other, more favorable, time.

SECRET KEY II: SPELLS

Part 2: Three Lusty Spells to Give You Total Physical Satisfaction

The Tantalizing New-Strength Spell

Before you retire for the night, place a piece of string about six inches long under your pillow. Perform this Spell just before you fall asleep.

As you relax in bed, turn on your back, straighten your body and slip your right hand under the pillow and touch the string.

Say aloud, [or in your head):

> "Powers of Sun and Moon and Light
> "Come to me in the still of night."

Pull the string from under your pillow, and hold it in front of your chest as you tie a single knot in it.

Say [or think]:

> "This knot shall raise me to a peak
> "Almighty strong – no longer weak."

Replace the string under your pillow, turn over and go to sleep.

Repeat this procedure on the following two nights. Then on the third morning, take the triple-knotted string from under your pillow and carry it with you wherever you go for the next 28 days.

This Spell works best if you started on the night of the New Moon.

The Occult Seduction Spell

For this Spell to work most efficiently you will need something which has been in contact with the person you wish to seduce. A hair or a fingernail clipping is best. Next best is a cigarette end or a tissue she [or he] has touched. This is called your contact object.

On the night of the New Moon, wait until you're reasonably sure the object of your lust is sleeping. Then sit in a darkened room and hold the contact object in your cupped hands against your breast.

Close your eyes, quietly say the name of the person you're lusting for, and **recite**:

> "Power of lust
> "Here are my sign
> "Naked feel
> "Your flesh to mine."

Really throw your heart and soul into that recitation – give it all you've got. Then wrap your contact object in a tissue and hold it in your hand as you retire for the night.

Carry this out on seven consecutive nights.

The Psychic Sex-Appeal Spell

After dark, turn out the light in your bathroom and stand a single lighted candle in a saucer in the bath. Find a picture of the person of the same sex as yourself whom you admire most in the world. Fix

SECRET KEY II: SPELLS

that picture at eye level on your bathroom mirror, using sticky tape to secure it.

Stand naked in front of the mirror, hands at your side and feet together. Stare at the picture.

Say:

> "By Powers and Forces from Above
> "I take from you the powers of love
> "Within myself I feel them grow
> "To overcome both friend and foe."

Then look into your own eyes in the mirror. Be relaxed, and blink when you need to – but continue to look into your own eyes for a full two minutes.

Then turn on the light, extinguish the candle, remove the picture from the mirror, and go about your business as usual.

Repeat this Spell as often as you please. Henceforward, when you meet or greet anyone you wish to impress, look at the bridge of his or her nose, between the eyes, for a few seconds. Don't make a big thing of it. If anyone says "What are you looking at me like that for?" you're over doing it.

Part 3: Three Vigorous Spells to Restore Your Health, Beauty and Potency.

Note:
These Spells must not be used as a substitute for recognized and regular medical treatment. They should be used only in conjunction with your doctor's diagnoses, recommendations and prescriptions. On no account tell any medical person that you are conducting these Spells, nor, when you are cured, tell anyone that Magic produced the cure.

The Tremendous Beauty-Is-Mine Spell

During the day, every hour on the hour [provided it is convenient, and that you will not attract attention to yourself], close your eyes and turn your face toward the sun.

Say [or think]:

> "Healing rays now begin
> "To bring new beauty pouring in."

Spend a few seconds considering how you would like to appear to others. Remember people you have admired, and think about what attributes of theirs would benefit you.

Start this Spell on the day following the Full Moon and continue for 28 days.

SECRET KEY II: SPELLS

The Stupendous Young-Again Spell

Find a photograph of yourself, taken when you were young and healthy. If you cannot find such a photograph, use instead a picture of any younger person of your sex who is obviously brimming with health and vitality.

Fill a glass with water and cover it with the saucer. Before noon, stand the glass on a window sill, preferably south-facing [or north-facing, if you live south of the equator]. Choose a clear day when the sun is shining.

At midnight [Full Moon is the best time] sit in a darkened room lit by a single candle on a table in front of you. Place your glass of water on the table to the right of the candle. Remove the saucer.

Relax in your chair, holding the photograph of yourself in both hands in your lap.

Lift the picture until it is illuminated by the light of the candle.

Look steadily at the picture.

Say:

> "Time reverse your steady flow,
> "In mind and body back I go
> "Far in the realms of space and plane
> "I drink at the Fountain of Youth again"

Put the picture down to the left of the candle, pick up the glass of water in your right hand and drink the water.

Repeat this Spell daily, as often as you wish.

The Exciting Brilliance-For-Me Spell

This Spell works best if it is first worked three days before the Moon is full, on a clear night when you can stand, either outside or at a window, with the moonlight shining on your face.

Stare at the silver disc of the Moon.

Solemnly say:

> "Luna, Luna, polished bright
> "Clean my mind, my soul, my sight.
> "Let a flame of brilliance grow
> All is clear. I see. I know."

Move to a comfortable chair, sit down and relax with your eyes closed for a minute. Then open a *non-fiction* book [not a magazine or a newspaper] at random and read for at least 10 minutes.

Stand up, face the Moon.

Say:

> "Luna, I thank Thee."

SECRET KEY II: SPELLS

Part 4: Four Dominating Spells to Give You Supreme Command Over Others

Note

If you feel uneasy about using any of these Spells, do not perform them. Use a suitable Ritual instead. More importantly, do *not* reveal by word, glance or deed that you are launching these Spells; as you will learn, there are defences against them, and your victim must be unaware of your intention, otherwise he or she may erect a protection, and your efforts will be wasted.

The Haunting Horror-Producing Spell

This Spell will strike unknown fears, anger and faulty judgement into whomever you aim it at. Do not use it on people you have to live with, or you may find their discord disturbing to your own peace of mind.

Carry out this Magic-working a day or two after New Moon when you are aware that your target is sleeping. Lie down on your bed and close your eyes.

Say:

> "The troubles and forces I send to thee
> "Shall never return to trouble me."

Now search in your mind for a memory of seeing or meeting the person you wish to work your Magic on. As soon as the memory is clear

Say:

> "Stir in your sleep and feel the effects
> "Of all that I send thee in the Name of this Hex.
> "From fiends of your mind shall your consciousness cower,
> Stir in thy brain as I pour in my Power."

As you finish saying the rhyme, recall the most frightening movie you've ever seen, or the scariest TV show you've watched. Then **say** the name of your target three times.

Follow that by **saying:**

> "Sealed with a Curse as sharp as a knife,
> Doomed are your plans and damned is your life."

Think of wet slimy things, crawling horrors, weird creatures, skeletons and evil smells slipping, slithering and dancing over your target as he or she lies sleeping.

Repeat his or her name three times more.

Say:

> "So shall it be."

Raise your right arm, point your forefinger at the ceiling and sign your name in the air, as if you were writing on an imaginary blackboard.

SECRET KEY II: SPELLS

Lie back down, think happy thoughts for yourself and drift off to sleep.

The Unseen Inner-Plane-Travel Spell

This Spell takes you to wherever you wish to be, to find out secrets.

Find a place and time were you can relax, lying comfortably full length. Decide where you wish to be or who you wish to spy on.

Take six slow deep breaths and **mentally repeat** seven times:

> "Distance, darkness, fade away
> "I seek the Mystic Traveling Ray.
> "Reveal before my mind's bright eye
> "The secrets which I wish to spy."

Relax physically, breathe easily and normally and close your eyes if they're not already closed. Think about where you wish to go. If you know the place, recall the last time you were there. If you're looking for a person, remember how that person was the last time you met.

Let your mind float free, think about your destination, and be comfortable. Each time you breathe in **say** the word "Relax" in your mind, and as you breathe out **think** the word "Travel." Let things happen, and do not resist the feelings of lightness and swaying which drift through your mind and body.

This Spell will likely take several workings before you get the knack of it, but sooner or later you will find that you *are* where you have been thinking, able to see and hear exactly what's going on there.

When you have found out what you wanted to know, your experience will slip into natural sleep and you will awake refreshed, with clear memories of what you went seeking.

The Crushing Disharmony-Exorcising Spell

This spell is designed to produce harmony between people who are at odds with each other. It can be used to such ends as stopping married couples from quarreling, or promoting mutual admiration between a boss and a worker.

It works best when performed unobtrusively in the presence of the people concerned.

Seat yourself where you can see the disagreeing parties. Look between, not at, them – with your gaze cutting across the emotional vibrations flashing backward and forward between them.

Then calmly **think** the following words:

> "In the Name above all other Names
> "I bring peace and harmonious aims
> "Replace war and strife
> "With cooperative life
> "Let the discord be burned up in flames."

As you are mentally reciting those words, envision that a clear white light is shining down, bathing the

SECRET KEY II: SPELLS

quarreling parties and yourself in its shaft of brilliance.

Repeat the spell whenever convenient, until they are harmonious.

The Staggering Return-Evil-To-Source Spell

This ancient Spell must be used only to avenge injuries or hurts which have been done to you. That is the *only* reason for working this Spell. If you use it against people you are jealous of, or simply because you dislike them, you stray away from the purpose of this Spell. It is designed to send the effects of the evil eye, Black Magic and hexes straight back to the person who is aiming them at you. What is being wished upon you will then happen to the sender instead. Work it when the Moon is full.

Take an apple and a sharp knife and place them on a table on each side of a candle. The knife should be on the right and the apple on the left. And ordinary white candle will do, but you can add greater power to the Spell if you use a brown one.

Sit at the table and concentrate on the person who is hexing you as you light the candle.

Say:

"Gadriel, I call Thee."

Pronounce his name "Gah-Drew-Ale," emphasizing the first syllable.

SECRET KEY II: SPELLS

Pick up the knife and cut the apple in half with one firm stroke, **saying**:

> "As this fruit is cut in two, so shall your evil return to you."

Say the name of your tormenter as you then extinguish the candle. Eat some of each piece of the apple, then bury the pieces of core, either in your garden or in the earth of a potted plant. If you have neither, throw the core into the garbage.

As you dispose of the core, **say**:

> "The torments being sent to me shall now return to......" [say the name of your tormentor.]

As the core rots away, your enemy will find that the evil Magic is being directed straight back to him or her. May it be enjoyed!

SECRET KEY II: SPELLS

Part 5: Three Personal Spells to Change Your Relationships for the Better

The New Opposition-Begone Spell

Here we have a Spell which knocks down general oppositions. If your life is not going ahead exactly as you would wish, yet you can't put your finger on what's wrong or who is standing in your way, this Spell may well open surprising avenues for you.

On the night of the New Moon, sweep under or around your bed and collect a little dust. Lay it carefully in the centre of a piece of plain white paper on a table where one candle burns. Put out all other lights.

Sit at the table and look at the flame of the candle.

Quietly say [or think]:

> "As this candle burns
> "As this planet turns
> "As this dust is scattered
> "My oppositions shatter."

As you finish saying the rhyme, carefully pick up the paper and blow the dust out of an open window.

Close the window, return to your seat at the table, look into the flame again.

Say:

> "Each day shall dawn
> "With a trouble gone.

"As fades this flame
"My troubles the same."

As you reach the word "same," blow the candle out. Sit for a minute in the dim before you switch on any light.

Repeat this Spell whenever you feel so inclined.

The Shattering Partnership-Disruption Spell

This vigorous little Spell is useful for breaking up undesirable partnerships. Perhaps you disapprove of one of your children's friends; maybe the love of your life is engaged to a rival and you feel you should separate them; or perhaps the disruption of a business partnership may seem to offer you advantages.

Note:
Marriages made before God have powerful Magical bonds which are extremely strong unless both partners agree to break them. Trying to disrupt an existing marriage by Magic is not only close to impossible, it's hazardous.

Obtain pictures of the parties you wish to separate. If they are together in one picture, so much the better. If you have two separate pictures, set them side by side and fix them together with transparent tape. If you are totally unable to obtain pictures, draw a sketch of them on paper. It doesn't matter whether or not you're artistic: only you are going to see the sketches, and you are aware of what the pictures are meant to represent. To further identify

SECRET KEY II: SPELLS

the sketches, write the names of the people under your drawings of them.

Two days after the Full Moon, at sunset, sit facing west with the picture [or pictures] on a table in front of you, along with a pair of scissors.

Hold the scissors closed, points upward, in front of your chest in your right hand.

Say:

> "These blades are together as are............ and............."
> [Here, say the names of the people involved in the partnership you wish to see broken].

Open the scissors, still with the points of upward.

Say:

> "These blades move apart, as shall.......... and............."
> [again, name the people].

Now cut the photograph(s) or drawing into two separate pieces, so that the people shown are broken apart. Spear one piece on each blade of the scissors. Hold the scissors with both hands, points upward, with the pictures impaled on them.

Say:

> "Cut apart. Cut asunder
> "Cut apart above and under
> "Broken shall these partners be

"By reason of the Powers of Three."

Take the pieces of photograph or paper, slide them together and cut them three times. Drop some of the pieces on the floor to your left and the rest to your right.

Say:

"Sun sink down below the rim
"Moon is waning back to dim,
"Turn the Cosmic Wheels of thought,
"The partnership shall fade to naught".

Stand up, pick up the pieces of picture and throw them in the garbage. Repeat the Spell on any convenient evening while the Moon is waning from Full toward New.

The Mighty Attackers-Confusion Spell

If you have people who are making your life uncomfortable through no fault of your own, then this Spell will confuse the minds of your enemies and their attacks will lose direction and force.

Take a piece of string about 12 inches long. Hang it out in the open for 24 hours. If it is within sight of your enemies as they pass by, so much the better.

At 8 p.m. on a convenient evening, sit yourself down alone, facing – as near as you can judge – toward your principal enemy's residence or room.

Tie a knot near the end of the string.

SECRET KEY II: SPELLS

Say:

> "Bind and twist; twist and bind,
> "This knot shall enter in her (his) mind."

Repeat this at 9 p.m. and 10 p.m., tying a new knot each time. Put the string outside again.

Carry out the Spell the following evening at the same times. Your string will now have six knots in it.

On the next evening, tie three more knots at the same hours, reciting the couplet as before.

When you have tied the ninth knot, tie the two ends of the string together. Take the twisted loop to a window and throw it out, **saying:**

> "Twined in tied; tied and twined,
> "Thoughts are twisted in her (his) mind.
> "As this twister rots away,
> "Shall her (his) reason lose its sway."

You will, of course, have been using the appropriate pronoun where the rhymes say "her" or "his." Once you have worked the Spell on your chief enemy, work it again on lesser foes.

Part 6: Five Practical Spells to Aid You in Your Job or Business Dealings

The Instant Business-Success Spell

Take three single cents and wrap them in a cloth.

Say:

> "Money, money let us see
> "Your powers flow from you to me."

Place the coins on a table and extend your writing hand above them, fingers together, palm down. Close your eyes and then point the forefinger of the same hand and write a large dollar sign three times in the air in front of you.

Say:

> "Golden showers, see them clear,
> "They grow and never disappear."

Open your eyes and unwrap the coins, **saying:**

> "These cents shall symbolize for me
> "A growing trade. So shall it be."

Mount the three coins on a triangular piece of cardboard or wood, and place them unobtrusively near your desk or cash drawer.

Never draw attention to them, but if someone asks what they are, you may say: "They're my good luck pieces."

SECRET KEY II: SPELLS

The Ancient Fame-And-Honors Spell

Use this Spell only if you are prepared to back it up with action. When it works, you will be required to appear in front of the public, to speak to reporters and television interviewers, and to make speeches.

Fame and honors carry responsibilities – make sure you're ready for them before you use this Spell to bring them to you.

You will need a head-and-shoulders photograph of yourself for this Spell, preferably a picture where you are looking directly at the camera.

As the New Moon is rising, sit alone in a darkened room with your photograph on a table in front of you.

Light two candles, one on each side of the photograph.

Stare fixedly at the picture of yourself.

Say:

> "By the Powers that govern
> "By the Force of the Name,
> "In the Sphere of Abraxas
> "I demand I find fame."

Continue to stare at the eyes in the photograph until it seems to float in a gray mist.

SECRET KEY II: SPELLS

Say:

> "ABRAXAS. ABRAXAS. ABRAXAS."
> (Pronounced "Ah-Bracks-Ass," emphasis on second syllable.)

Extinguish the candles. Lift your head, close your eyes, and stare *through* your eyelids. Sit perfectly still and feel a tingling begin in your fingers and hands, which should be resting in your lap.

Raise your hands in front of you, fingers spread, palms turned towards your face.

Say:

> "These hands, this mind and this body shall, in the name of Abraxas, attract honors and fame. So shall it be."

Replace your hands in your lap and relax for a minute. Then stand and announce what fame and honors you are seeking, just as if you were introducing yourself to an audience of thousands.

Repeat this Spell each evening and during your day-to-day life; be prepared to except the opportunities which Fate offers you. Hanging back at any time will mitigate the force of the Spell and delay its results.

The Fantastic Win-At-Law Spell

Perform this Spell at midnight before any Court appearance.

SECRET KEY II: SPELLS

Place the papers associated with your legal battle on a table. Place a candle to the right of them.

Exactly at midnight light the candle. Sit at the table and as the candle burns brightly, study the flame closely.

When it is burning clearly and steadily, stare into the flame. Lay your writing hand on the papers and think about whatever result you are hoping for.

Then say:

>"Rash of Mithra hear me!
>"My cause is right and true,
>"Influence the powers that judge,
>"I ask this boon of you."

Stand up and walk three times around your chair, to the right. Sit down again, lay your hand on the papers and stare into the candle flame. The flame will be moving now: sit still until it steadies.

Say:

>"Rash of Mithra, I thank Thee for Thy aid against .... [name your opponents].

Extinguish the candle, turn on the lights and before the candle cools, carefully pour a little of the liquid wax onto a piece of plain paper. Fold the paper and let it cool before putting it under your pillow for the night.

In the morning write the name 'RASH OF MITHRA' on the paper and keep it with you during the day.

Keep it out of sight, however, and destroy it after your law case is settled.

The Glorious Move-Up-In-Life Spell

Like similar Spells, you must know what you want to be or where you want to go before you apply the powerful Magic described here. There is no need for you to know *how* this will be accomplished – let the Cosmic Powers look after that – but you must formulate clear ideas of what you wish to accomplish.

Once you have decided what your move up in life is going to be, collect three or four photographs [probably cut out of newspapers or magazines] of people enjoying the conditions which you're aiming to reach.

On any night, when the Moon is between New and Full – that is, waxing – lay your photographs on a table. Place a large pinch of salt on a piece of paper to the left of the pictures, and a candle to the right.

Arrange things so that as you sit before the table you are facing east.

Light the candle, extinguish all other lights, and sit down at the table. Look toward the eastern horizon. There will probably be a wall of the room in the way, but stare through it as if you were watching a scene far away from you.

SECRET KEY II: SPELLS

Say:

> "O Spiritual Sun whose visible symbol
> "Rises from this place,
> "Witness my desire to rise and shine
> "On those below, as does your face."

Look down at the pictures. Examine them, lean forward and breathe on them. Pick up a pinch of salt and sprinkle it over the pictures.

Say:

> "Creature of Earth, adore these beings.
> "Link my destiny with theirs.
> "Offer chances to me – which I promise to take,
> "To move forward and upward toward my desires."

Continue to study the pictures closely. Take in every detail, then sit back and close your eyes. Stand up slowly and raise your arms to their fullest extent above your head, fingers apart and your palms facing forward.

Say:

> "I call on the Lords of Karma
> "To hear my demand.
> "Give me the chances
> "And I'll take command."

Sit down again, put your hands in your lap. Open your eyes and extinguish the candle. Sit quietly in the dark for a few minutes pretending that you have already moved up in life as you requested. Plan what you will do with your life when your desires have been granted.

Repeat this Spell three times more before the Moon is Full.

The Wonderful Money-Aid Spell

Obtain the largest denomination dollar bill you can afford. Take an envelope, fold the bill once and seal it inside the envelope.

Keep the envelope in the same room with you at all times for the next seven days.

At convenient times, as often as you wish, place the envelope against your forehead.

Say [or think]:

> "Occult powers to me shall bring
> "The way to double this sum,
> "Hear me, thou Cherubim which sing,
> "Quickly and softly come."

As you move the envelope away from your forehead, pretend that it is heavier and bulkier than before. Think about what you need extra cash for, and exactly how much you want. Then dismiss the Spell from your mind until you are ready to repeat it.

Be totally alert during your day-to-day life for every opportunity offered to you which will enhance your worth.

SECRET KEY II: SPELLS

At the end of seven days, unseal the envelope and either spend the money on essentials or put it back in the bank. If you need to repeat the Spell, use a different bill.

SECRET KEY II: SPELLS

Part 7: Six Exclusive Spells to Solve Your Life Problems

The Startling Come-From-Above Spell

This Spell calls disembodied entities from the Inner Planes to assist you. While the forces you are commanding are good and helpful, I suggest you practice with other Spells and Rituals before you try this one. It can produce results which are startling to people who have never investigated occult areas.

Also, if you have ever had psychiatric treatment for delusions, illusions, voices in your head or any other hallucinatory tendencies, I advise you not to use this Spell: not because of any danger, but simply because the results will be unreliable for you.

The best time to work this Spell is on the night of the Full Moon, between midnight and 1 a.m. You will also get satisfactory results between 9 p.m. and midnight on Sundays.

Preparations are simple, but you need to ensure silence with no interruptions. How you manage that is up to you: if you find yourself constantly interrupted when you attempt this Spell, you should recognize that mystic reasons are the cause. Probably you should attempt some other means of finding what you seek – take a look at other Spells and Rituals: you'll surely find something to fit your requirements.

Note:
If your doctor advises you that deep breathing is dangerous for you [and that will usually apply to

SECRET KEY II: SPELLS

anyone who has a heart condition]; or if at any time during this Magic-working you become dizzy or see spots dancing before your eyes, do not continue with this Spell.

First **memorize** the following invocation, because you need to be able to repeat it with your eyes closed:

> "I seek the good spirits of the Inner Planes
> "The information I receive will be used only for good.
> "I ask that honest spirits communicate with me.
> "Grant that I shall gain truth and understanding from them."

Lie down comfortably on your bed with your head to the north if possible. Close your eyes. Breathe deeply for several minutes. As you inhale, **think** the word "Relax" and each time you exhale **think** "Deeper". Keep this going until the tingling which will begin in your hands goes away.

Let your breathing return to normal, and then **say** the above invocation three times, in your mind, not aloud.

Then, quietly, **say** the Angelic Name HAHAIAH, which is pronounced "Ha-ha-ee-yah" with the emphasis on the second syllable. Repeat the Name about 10 times, then lie quietly for a few minutes.

Let your brain idle. Stay relaxed and listen to the silence. Particularly listen for faint whispers or rustling which may reach you.

Then, in your mind ask a question. One question, briefly and concisely. Make it a serious question – nothing flippant. If you make fun of the entities during this Spell, you'll merely get confusing replies.

So state the question in your mind, and then let your brain go quiet again. Pay attention to the tiniest wisps of sound, voices or murmurs which occur around you. If you cannot distinguish words, quietly think: "Repeat, please."

Then lie still again and listen. Now, if no sounds reach you, *try listening to your mind*. Sometimes the communicating entity will "talk" to you by inserting a train of thought into your mind. So after you request the repetition, be aware of answers coming into your mind as thoughts of unknown origin.

You are opening up a channel of communication which has likely been closed off for years, so this Spell may take a few workings before the "line" is clear, as "tuning in" can take a little while. But once you have built a firm contract, you will be given startling knowledge by this means.

The Expansive Bring-Me-Excitement Spell

If your life is dull and uninteresting, this is the Spell which can alter all that.

You will need to collect some things which you associate with stimulating conditions. If you are looking for stage entertainment, then used movie or theatre tickets stubs are what you should seek. If you want to travel, then bus, train or plane tickets are your goals. Want to be invited to parties? Find

SECRET KEY II: SPELLS

some party favors or similar mementoes. The whole idea is to accumulate items which have been involved with the excitement you lack.

Carry out this Spell at any time, noon or night. Arrange your 'excitement items' in a two foot circle on the floor. Dress yourself in clothes appropriate to the entertainment you seek and try to include at least one garment of red or orange. For example, if it's a ball game you're looking for, dress yourself for a stay in the bleachers; traveling – suitable outdoor clothes; and if skinny dipping is your target...well, you've got no problem about what to wear for that!

Stand in the circle of 'excitement items,' facing east. Stand up straight with your hands loose at your sides.

Say:

> "In the names of Cassiel and Shatiel, bring excitement into my life."

Turn around to your right so that you are facing west. Raise your right hand and point your forefinger upward.

Say:

> "Hear me call, hear my plea,
> "Stimulation come to me."

Turn to your right again until you are facing east. Lower your hands to your side.

Say:

> "I ask this in the Names of Cassiel, who knows of solitude, and Shatiel, who knows of silence."

Those Angelic Names are pronounced "Kah-See-Ale" and "Shah-Tee-Ale," both with the emphasis on the third symbol.

Bend down and pick up the 'excitement items' and put them on a shelf where you can see them. Repeat this Spell for the next six days, or until life has become stimulating enough for you – whichever comes first.

The Certain Danger-Stay-Away Spell

This quick and easy Spell can be used at any time danger threatens. It invariably reduces the impact of the danger and can change an impending fatality to a less calamitous outcome, or even avert the danger altogether.

When danger threatens, surround yourself with powerful protective influences.

By saying [or thinking] three times:

> "Pedael, protect me"

Pronounce His Name "Pay-Dah-Ale," with the emphasis on the final syllable.

SECRET KEY II: SPELLS

The Brilliant Travel-Safely Spell

This is another simple Spell which brings powerful protective influences to you.

To ensure a safe journey or to turn malignant travel influences to less harmful ones,

Say [or think] three times:

> "Susabo, stay with me on my journey."

Pronounce His Name "Soo-Sah-Bo" with the emphasis on the second syllable.

If, while invoking this protection, you are holding a piece of blue cloth or paper, you will reinforce the protection.

The Protective Magic-Away Spell

If you are certain that someone is sending black magic or the evil eye against you, use this Spell.

Cut out a circular piece of white paper about 3 inches in diameter. Write your attacker's name on the paper in red ink and draw a circle around it.

Say, putting force behind your words:

> "Evil return to source
> "Impelled by incredible Force.
> "In the name of Tobiit
> "I'm protected. So be it."

Point your right forefinger at the paper as you say that. You'll have no problem with pronouncing the Angel's Name – those last two lines rhyme perfectly.

Carry the paper with you at all times, and your attacker's attempts to harm you will fly back to him or her.

The Reliable Know-The-Unknown Spell

Floating in this Universe is a vast a pool of surprising information and useful knowledge which anyone can draw on through the magic of this Spell. Just as you are drifting off to sleep,

Say three times:

"Raphael, bring me secret knowledge."

Pronounce His Name "Rah-Fay-Ale," with the emphasis on the last syllable.

Keep a notebook and pencil beside your bed and make a brief record of your dreams *as soon as you wake up in the morning.* More importantly, if you wake in the night, think about what you have been dreaming and make a note of it before you go back to sleep.

You will find that facts which may assist you in improving your life will become known to you in your dreams. Use the knowledge to your own advantage.

Secret Key III: RITUALS

Twenty Seven Masterly Rituals To Magnificently Remodel Your Total Existence

Rituals are the ultimate in Magic. Their patterns and vibrations, which you control, plant irresistible commands in the Cosmos, and the mighty Cosmic Beings you call on automatically swing into action to satisfy your needs.

Over the centuries, thousands of Rituals have been discovered. The twenty seven Rituals which follow in this Grimoire are the final distillation, the ultimate selection of the most powerful, most effective and most useful Rituals ever gathered between two covers. Weaker, less effective Rituals were rejected in favor of this time-tested, supremely majestic, unparalleled group of unsurpassable Rituals, carefully selected to cover every eventuality you could wish.

During the 30 years of research and testing which were carried out before this book could be released with a certainty that it carried the ultimate efficient power to help anyone transform his or her life, I made a fantastic discovery.

All genuine Rituals – the cream of the Magical crop which are in this book – are basically alike in structure. Testing literally thousands of Rituals, discarding those which did not come up to high standards of perfection and simplicity, I found that only eight simple variables made any Ritual differ from another.

A variety of special key words were needed to begin a

SECRET KEY III: RITUALS

Ritual; naturally, the purposes varied; the ruling planets were different; particular Cosmic Beings controlled their own areas of authority; the proposed aims of the operator were unique; a specialized phrase was needed to fix the Cosmic Powers on their target; one of the 12 Talismans was needed; and most Rituals had maximum power on a particular day, between certain times.

But apart from those eight variable factors, the remaining details of these top flight Rituals are identical. What a simple and satisfying prospect opened up from that revelation! I could write a Master Procedure for all the Rituals, leaving spaces to insert the eight varying details. That Master Procedure follows, and the eight key details for each Ritual are listed in Parts 3 through 9.

What could be simpler? You follow the simple steps of the Master Procedure, dropping the eight special details into place like keys into locks as you go.

The Cosmic Beings will then arrange your future to bring your commands to reality. You, of course, will respond to their effects by reacting to the opportunities which miraculously appear, and you will handle the physical arrangements where necessary.

For instance, when Purah finds you a new home after you have worked the Ideal Change-My-Home Ritual, you will take the necessary steps to move your furniture and to handle any paperwork involved.

Magic is a two way street. The Cosmic Beings will bring opportunities your way in abundance – it is

SECRET KEY III: RITUALS

your task to grab those opportunities and act on them. For example, if you work the Thrilling I-Can-Wow-Them Ritual for success on the stage, and then lock yourself away in your room, you are deliberately opposing the Magic.

So after you work a Ritual, make efforts to place yourself in the way of positive results. That's a small point which many Magic Workers are not aware of, and it's important to the ultimate, shining success of your future life of plenty, harmony and happiness.

Follow the steps indicated in the ensuing pages, and join the exultant, secret clique who know that with Magic you can achieve every glorious detail of your deepest needs.

SECRET KEY III: RITUALS

Part 1: Initial Preparations to Focus the Illustrious Cosmic Powers

Once you have decided which Ritual you will work, you can begin on the simple preparations. Step by easy step, you make a place to work and tune in to the Cosmic Powers, preparing yourself and proceeding with the actual Magic working.

Each step is carefully explained, and you will need nothing which you cannot easily find in your home. All the other magical ingredients are here in this book.

Every Ritual revealed to you requires the same physical conditions: the only differences are in the Words and gestures you use as you perform the Ritual.

Rituals Change Your Life Effortlessly

Working Rituals is easy. Over the years all kinds of confusions have been added, but in reality working Magic is simpler than baking a cake.

In fact, working a Ritual is remarkably similar to baking a cake. In the kitchen, if you're setting out to bake, you clear a space to work in, you try to make sure you're not disturbed by callers, you gather the ingredients, mix them, then pop the mixture in the oven and go away and leave it.

Magic is just the same – with the added advantage that if any of the ingredients happen not to be available, you can leave them out and still have an

SECRET KEY III: RITUALS

excellent chance of everything turning out as you wish.

The only difference between baking a cake and working a Ritual is that a great deal of Magic consists of Words and gestures in place of flour, eggs and sugar!

Clearing Your Working Space

If your kitchen was filled with children, domestic animals, casual callers, surplus furniture, dirty dishes and wet laundry you'd have to be a remarkably well organized person to hope to turn out a successful recipe under those conditions.

So the first thing you would do to ensure success would be to clear a working surface, hustle everyone out for awhile, and then get to work.

You need to do exactly that for your Magic-working. First, by making a physical space to stand in without being obstructed or cluttered, and second, by making a 'mind space' by using certain words and gestures which move obstructive thoughts and influences away for a while.

Clear An Area To Use For Your Magic

Find some corner of your home where you can shift the furniture, leaving a standing space for you about six feet square. That means when you stand at the center of your cleared area, the walls and furniture are at least 3 feet away from you all around. If you can arrange this space in the east side or eastern corner of a room, so much the better.

SECRET KEY III: RITUALS

You're going to need one single piece of furniture in your Magical working space. That will be your altar, and the simplest altar in the world is an empty orange crate. Anything will do which gives you a flat surface about two feet long by a foot wide to put your Magical ingredients on.

Some people use a small coffee table, but I've seen a wooden board spanning a couple of bricks used very successfully. When you've decided what you're going to use for your altar, place it in the east end of your cleared area with the long dimension of your altar running approximately north and south. That means that as you stand in front of your altar you will be facing the east, where the sun rises in September or March. If you want to be really fussy about this you can use a hiker's compass to locate your altar.

VcToria Notes: that all cell phones now have a compass.

The Four Elemental Amulets On Your Altar

While you are working your Rituals, you are focusing Mystic Energies which vibrate along the same lines as the earth, air, fire and water you will be speaking of as you make your preparations.

Your altar should carry items representing those four elements.

In the Amulet kit that is supplied with this book you will find illustrations of four Elemental Amulets which were created and drawn by a close associate of mine, a powerful Secret Brother of the Magical

SECRET KEY III: RITUALS

Fraternity and Order of which we are privileged to be members.

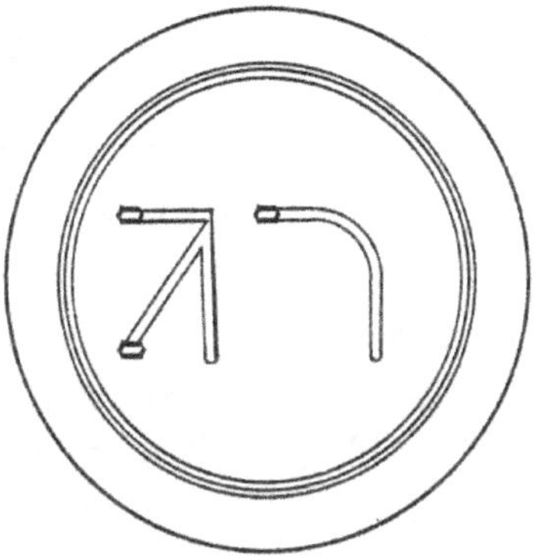

EARTH 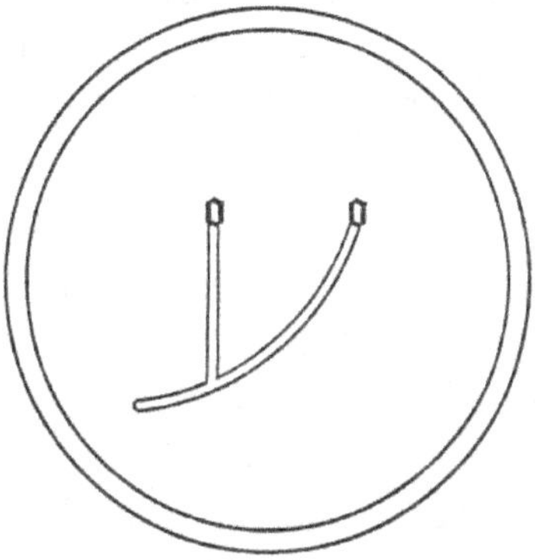   **AIR**

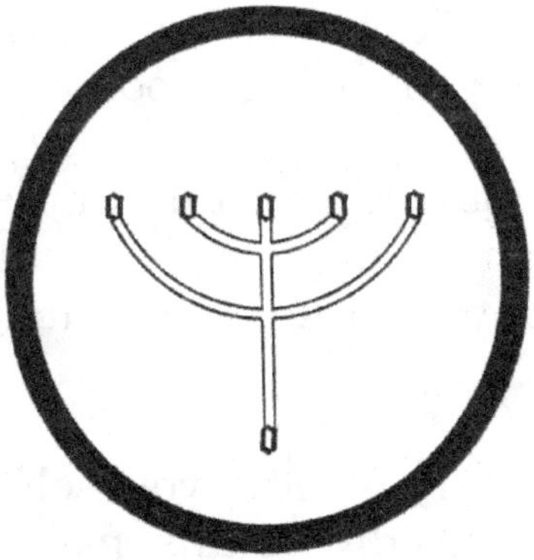

FIRE 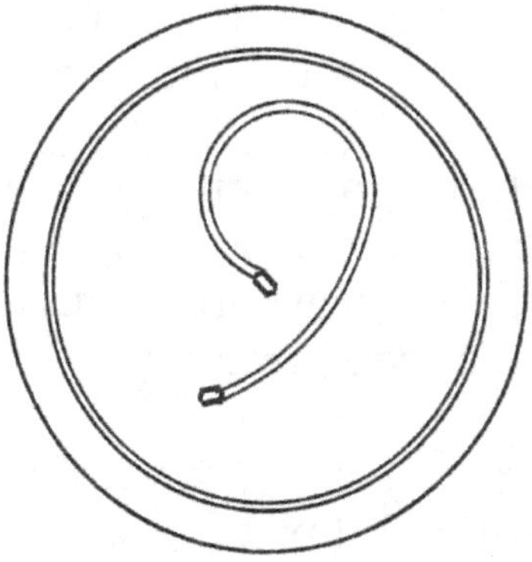   **WATER**

If your book does not contain the Elemental Amulate Kit you may order them from the web store at: www.alternativeuniverse.ca. These kits come impressed with the energy of Frater Malak, who, although he resides on the other side, frequently channels to his daughter who rewrote this book. During channeling she asks that the kits be infused

SECRET KEY III: RITUALS

with the original energy that is need to work the Rituals.

There is only one way of creating the Elemental Amulet for your altar. It is to use the special Mystic Grimoire Talisman and Amulet Kit.

Note: In the original book that Frater Malak wrote he drew pictures of the Four Elemental Amulets. He also wrote that they had no magical purpose. They did not have the necessary occult energy impressed into them. Therefore since each book ordered directly from www.alternativeuniverse.ca webstore has the Kit I saw no need to include these pages.

If you have ordered from any other source, you need to purchase the Talisman Kit from the website above. It is not included in the cost of the book.

Taking your kit with the four Elemental Amulets carefully cut out each of them from pages three and five. Use scissors to cut smoothly around the outside line of each amulet.

The Kit is the power of source. Prove it to yourself by sitting, relaxed, and staring fixedly at any page in the Kit. See how the sigils seem to move and glow with an energy of their own.

If you wish you could make these Elemental Amulets more permanent by sticking each one on a piece of cardboard. Alternatively, if convenient, you can glue the Amulets directly to the surface of your altar.

A third alternative is to get yourself a supply of the Kits from his daughter who owns The Alternative

SECRET KEY III: RITUALS

Universe: www.alternativeuniverse.ca, so that as your Amulets become worn or soiled, you always have sparkling fresh ones at hand. That choice is yours.

To add further power to them, your amulets may be colored, although this is not absolutely necessary. Use any means you wish to color them, such as watercolors, wax pencils, oil paints, felt pens or inks – but be very careful not to obscure the black sigils and other markings on them.

The Earth Amulet should be shaded in with earth color – a warm brown.

The Air Amulet should be colored light blue.

The Fire Amulet should be colored red or bright orange.

The Water Amulet should be colored light green.

Use them as they are printed if you wish – but coloring them will repay the slight effort needed a hundred fold in the extra power generated in your Rituals.

When you have created them, place them on top of your altar.

The Air Amulet is laid at the back of the altar, in the centre. The Water Amulet is placed near the front, the Fire Amulet to the right, and the Earth Amulet on the left.

SECRET KEY III: RITUALS

Frater Malak and the Altar

SECRET KEY III: RITUALS

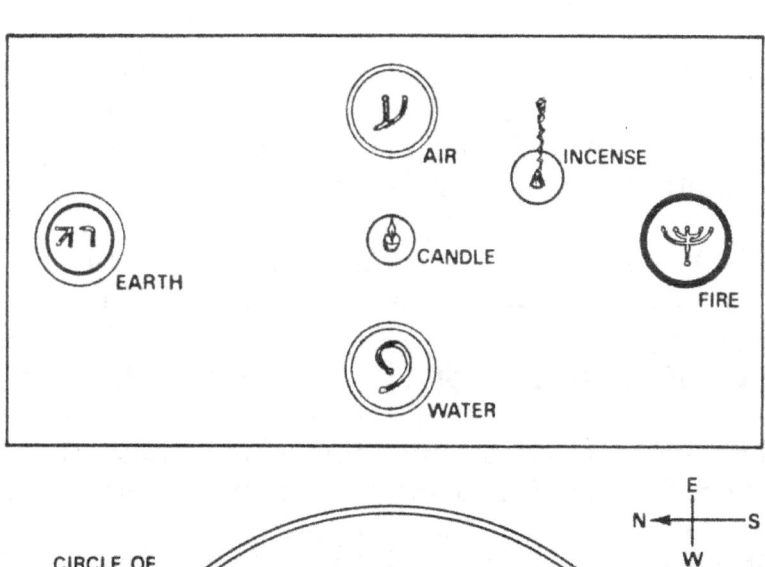

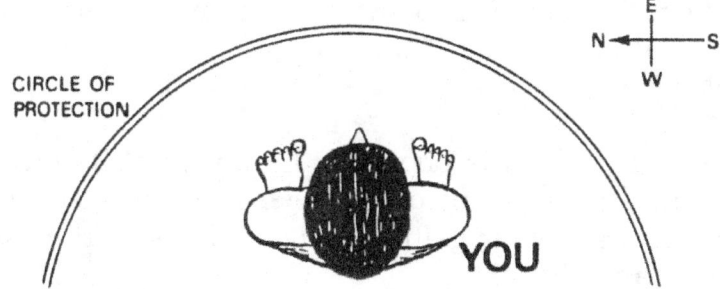

SECRET KEY III: RITUALS

The Mystic Flame

Rituals require you to burn a candle on your altar. It is known as the Mystic Flame.

For convenience, use a saucer, bottle or candlestick to hold the candle.

The same candle can be used over and over again until it is consumed, when you will replace it with a fresh one. An ordinary white kitchen candle is perfectly suited to Ritual working.

Your Mystic Flame stands at the centre of the altar unless the particular Ritual instructs you otherwise.

The Thaumaturgic Triplet

Don't be alarmed at the complicated name of this important focusing point for Cosmic Energies. An illustration of this Thaumaturgic Triplet is shown below.

The picture in this book has no power of its own, so cutting it out is not only useless, it will also defeat any hopes of your gaining magical benefit from these Spells and Rituals.

Thus, you must use the power-charged Triplet on page 7 in the 'Mystic Grimoire Talisman Amulet Kit,' cutting it out carefully.

This Triplet will also benefit from being colored, if you wish to take the time and make the effort.

The triangle in the center should be coloured bright

red; the three sections of the circle outside the triangle should be bright blue, and the four corners which remain outside the circle should be coloured light yellow.

As with the Elemental Amulets, this coloring is not absolutely necessary, but if you can accomplish it, the colors will add great energy to your Rituals.

Once created, secure the Triplet to a convenient wall at eye level, near your altar.

Circle Of Protection

A piece of rope, twine or string about 3 yards long maybe used to make a circle on the floor in front of your altar for you to stand in.

If you use rope, it should be flexible and not too thick. String will suit admirably, as long as it is not so thin that you have difficulty seeing it when it is laid on the floor.

See the diagram of the Altar to place your rope.

Expurgating Smoke

Incenses which are burned during Rituals are for the purpose of expelling unneeded vibrations from the vicinity of your altar. Any incense will do the work.

Place your incense in any convenient holder, or even on the lid of an old tin can. Just take care to see that no fire hazard is created, and remember that incense sticks drop light ash from the top.

Incense stands on the right side of your altar, between the Fire and Air Amulets.

Note: If you suffer from any breathing or pulmonary conditions which make smoke objectionable, uncomfortable or dangerous for you, dispense with the incense and ignore all references to it during the Rituals. The Cosmic Beings will understand and make allowances, just as they will for any other enforced or unintentional omissions from your Rituals.

Your Magical Working Space Is Complete

On your altar are the Four Elemental Amulets, your Mystic Flame and Incense ready to burn. The Thaumaturgic Triplet is on the wall, and your Circle of Protection rope or string is at hand.

SECRET KEY III: RITUALS

Next, prepare yourself. Just as you put on particular clothes to go outside, and wear other clothes [or none at all] to go to bed, so Magic Working has its own style of dress for you.

It's all quite simple. You need three things only: a Psychic Cloak, some Magical Oil, and Mystic Talisman. Don't worry – none of them are in the least difficult to obtain.

Your Psychic Cloak

A dressing gown, a light topcoat or any other similar garment will make your Psychic Cloak. Use an old piece of clothing which you rarely wear, loose enough for you to raise your arms above your head. The color or material is not vastly important, although it might be better if you can steer away from dull brown.

This will be the only garment you will wear during your Rituals and when you have decided which one you're going to use, carry out the following Power Induction one time only. This makes certain that when you put on your Psychic Cloak, the right Forces are tuned in.

Psychic Cloak Power Induction

After sundown, strip completely, removing your jewelry, wristwatch, necklace, earrings, pendants, and any other ornamentation you are wearing. However, if you have a wedding band or other adornment which you *never* remove – either from sentiment or because of physical difficulties with knuckle joints – leave it in place.

SECRET KEY III: RITUALS

Put on your Psychic Cloak garment and face west, where the sun has gone down.

Say:

"This garment I name my Psychic Cloak.
"Witness my words, Morael.
"In the Name which is above every other Name
"I wear this Cloak for good."

The Angel's Name is pronounced "Moe-Rah-Ale" with the emphasis on the final symbol.

How To make Your Magical Oil

Grapes have long been known to possess arcane powers and they form the basis of your Magical Oil which is used during all Rituals.

In a cup or glass slowly squeeze three choice grapes. Sprinkle a little salt into the container, and add a tablespoon full of vegetable oil. Olive, peanut, corn, cottonseed, sesame seed, poppy seed....any type of oil used in cooking is perfect.

Add some more grapes, press the mixture down with a spoon and sprinkle in more salt. Then add a tablespoon of oil. Continue this until the container is almost full. Cover it with a saucer or suitable lid and put it away in a dark and cool place for 24 hours.

At the end of that time, pour the mixture through a cloth or sieve into a convenient bottle or jar which has a cork or lid. Discard the used grape pulp. Label this container so you do not inadvertently use your Magical Oil for cooking.

SECRET KEY III: RITUALS

Bless your Magical Oil as follows. You need to repeat this Blessing only when you make a fresh supply of oil. Put your oil container on your altar. Stand before it and

Say:

> "Creature of the Elements,
> "You are created for me
> "To focus the Forces of Good.
> "Be blessed in the Name of the Highest."

Your Mystic Talismans

During every Ritual you will wear a Mystic Talisman on your chest. The 12 Mystic Talismans come with your kit, The Mystic Grimoire Talisman and Amulet Kit. For the diagrams, see below.

Just in case you may have skipped previous sections, and because it is such a vital point, I repeat: no illustrations in this book carries occult powers – these have been impressed into the Amulets, Triplet and Talismans in the 'Mystic Grimoire Talisman and Amulet Kit' which accompanies this Grimoire when bought directly from www.alternativeuniverse.ca.

If bought elsewhere the Talisman Kit is not included and needs to be purchased from the website above.

Where the Elemental Amulets are described, if you have missed this piece of critical information, in five words: **DO NOT CUT THIS BOOK.**

SECRET KEY III: RITUALS

SECRET KEY III: RITUALS

To get these 12 Talismans shown on the previous page they are in the Talisman Kit that only comes with the book if it is bought directly from www.alternativeuniverse.ca. If you obtained the book elsewhere, you need to go to the website mentioned, and purchase the Talisman Kit that can be bought with the impressed Magical energy that is needed to work the Rituals in this book.

If you bought the book elsewhere you can buy the Talisman Kit from the website above. You must cut them from the Kit. Tracing or machine copying them absolutely will not work.

When you have created your Talismans, pierce a hole near the edge of each where shown, and make a string halter for each one so that you can wear them like pendants. The strings should be adjusted to a length at which the center of the Talisman hangs about 4 inches above your navel.

Your Preparations Are Complete

You now have all your need for any of your Rituals. The steps you take after this are all actually part of the Rituals themselves, even though they take place before the Magic working is brought to a peak of glittering power which changes your least problems into ecstatic successes and joy.

SECRET KEY III: RITUALS

Part 2: The Master Procedure Which Commands the Mystic Beings to Bring Your Goals into Brilliant Reality

In Parts 3 through 9 of this Secret Key you will find the details of the 27 magnificent Rituals which are yours to bring you joy, harmony and riches. You are informed when to perform your Magic; the Password which will open the Doors to the Planes; how to announce the purpose of your Call; what Planets are represented; the Name of the Cosmic Being who carries out your wishes; how to state what you want; and the Avatar Mantrum, a simple phrase which sets the seal of success on your Ritual.

All these Rituals have a basic form which is easily understood and applied, so to save repeating instructions which are common to each Ritual, this Secret Key gives you the framework of Magic-Working.

Thus all you need to do is to turn to the page giving the eight inner details of the Ritual you wish to work, and then apply them in the order shown here.

This method of step-by-step Magic Working is unique, new and efficient. Never before has anyone ever had such a simple way of following in the steps of the Ancient Magicians. Follow the instructions as easily as if you were opening a package of cornflakes, and your startling, shining Miracles will follow, as surely as day follows night.

Modifying These Details Will Not Interrupt the Titanic Power of Your Magic Working

Remember that the details given here are suggestions for working Magic under ideal conditions. If you can fulfill all these conditions, you will be aligned with the maximum possible effect of the Cosmic Powers; but as I pointed out to you before, ignoring any detail will only slightly cut back the power of a Ritual – and all of these have power to spare for achieving their thrilling objectives.

Conditions for Assured Success In Magic Working

Before starting to work a Ritual, you should observe as many of the following conditions as are practical for you.

I say 'practical' because as you know, you should not alter your normal way of life, or attract undue attention to yourself with Magic. It works best when you keep it secret from others, so you should apply the following suggestions only as far as they will not have you publicly behaving in an abnormal manner.

Obviously, if you are a working person – and remember Magic can change all that for you very soon – conditions 3 and 4 below may be difficult for you to observe, for instance.

So start your Magical Works by following as many of these simple steps as you can without upsetting your regular routine. In particular, you should consult your doctor to find out whether the suggested 12-hour fast will be dangerous to your health.

SECRET KEY III: RITUALS

1. Decide on the time you will be working your Ritual. [Best times are indicated as Item 7 in the Ritual details in Parts 3 through 9, but modify those times as you wish, to suit your personal routine].

2. For 12 hours before the start of the Ritual, abstain from food and sex.

3. During those 12 hours, drink only water for the first 6 hours, and take a glass of wine or pure fruit juice when you need it during the second six hours. In particular, do not take any cola drinks throughout that time (i.e., drinks with fizz).

4. Stay alert and awake during those 12 hours. No catnaps.

5. During the final hour before you begin the Ritual, speak to no one. If you have to break your silence because the telephone rings or someone needs your attention, that does not matter: just keep the conversation short and to the point as feasible. This can be the most challenging time of all, as you try to act normally and keep secret your intentions. *On no account say to your caller "I've got to let you go now because it's time for me to start a Magic Ritual"* or any similar statement which might reveal what you are doing. That will uncover your secret and put a heavy damper on all your future Magical operations. Should you decide, because of unavoidable interruptions, that you have totally broken your Hour of Silence, postpone your Ritual to an hour later, and try to keep silent for that hour instead. Always remember that when you encounter frequent obstacles to starting or completing a Ritual, it is likely to be happening because Mystic Beings are

telling you to conduct the Ritual at some other time. You'll never be told "Don't work that Ritual now" by any of the Cosmic Forces, because they will never interfere with your freewill decisions. But a whole raft of delays, interruptions and hitches in a Ritual will clearly convey to you the message that you would do better to try again later.

6. At the beginning of your Hour of Silence, take a shower, bath or wash down. Then rub your chest, buttocks, hands and knees with a few drops of your Magical Oil.

7. Five minutes before Ritual starting time, strip completely and put on your Psychic Cloak. Remove all jewelry as you did when you blessed the Cloak.

8. Lastly, take the correct Mystic Talisman for the particular Ritual, and hang it on your breast. Item 8 in the Ritual details tells you which Talisman to use.

Working your Chosen Ritual Which Brings Your Personal Miracles Automatically

Your Place of Working is prepared, and you are ready to proceed.

Lay your Rope of Protection in a circle on the floor in front of your altar leaving the two ends about 12 inches apart.

Light the altar candle and extinguish all other lights. Step within the circle of your Rope of Protection and close it by tying the two ends together or overlapping them on the floor.

SECRET KEY III: RITUALS

You have begun. The Cosmic Wheels are already turning, and you are about to bring whatever you wish cascading into your life – money, love, health, virility, the disappearance of trouble...anything. You are going to name it, and it shall be so.

You're Working Your Magic, So Here Comes Happiness and Plenty

You're now standing before your altar, ready to start. Your next step is to clean out unneeded mental vibrations.

Any room, even in a brand new house, is filled with vibrations left over from the minds of people who lived in the room, or built the house, or even just passed through.

Your task, before calling down the Cosmic Beings, is to push all the unnecessary vibrations out of the way. You do it simply and easily with the following words and gestures.

The Place-Cleaning Ritual

Note:
Until you can easily recall this Ritual and the words, you can hold this book open in your left hand, consulting it as necessary.

Stand inside your Circle of Protection facing east, about two feet from your altar: feet together, hands at your sides, fingers relaxed. Close your eyes and raise your right hand above your head and point your forefinger at the ceiling.

Say:

>"You are."

With your arm straight, swing your hand down in front of you until you are pointing at the floor between your feet.

Say:

>"This Universe."

Still pointing with your finger, bend your elbow and bring your hand up until you are pointing at your right shoulder.

Say:

>"The Power."

Move your hand across your chest and point at your left shoulder.

Say:

>"And the Glory."

Bring both hand palms together, to your chest in an attitude of prayer. [If you were holding this book, lay your right palm flat against it as you raise your hands to your chest.]

Say:

>"For ever. So be it."

SECRET KEY III: RITUALS

Return your left hand to your side, and point directly in front of you with your right hand, just as if you were pointing at a ship on the far horizon. Move your right forefinger *only* in a small clockwise circle. As you do that

Say:

> "Tetra."
> (That pronunciation rhymes with 'wet fur').

Now turn slowly half right, still with your hand stuck out level in front of you. Stop turning as you face south. Make the same small circle with your finger.

Say:

> "Gram." (Rhymes with 'ham').

Make another quarter turn to your right, so that you are facing west and repeat the finger circle as you

Say:

> "Mut." (Rhymes with 'cut').

Turn to the north, make your fourth finger circle.

Say:

> "Ton." (Rhymes with 'gone').

Finally, turn right until you are facing east where you started.

SECRET KEY III: RITUALS

Raise both your hands above your head about two feet apart, with your fingers straight and palms facing forward. Your position is like a capital Y.

Say:

> "In front of me is Air Energy; behind me is Water Energy; on my right side is Fire Energy; and on my left side is Earth Energy. Around me shine the circles and above me shines the Light of Power."

Now turn around to your right so that your back is to the altar and you are facing west, still with your hands raised.

Announce:

> "I send from this place all intruding forces. They shall go far away, and be powerless to interfere with my wishes. So be it."

Turn to your right again, facing the altar and lower your hands to your sides, relaxing your fingers. Light the incense after opening your eyes.

You have now 'cleaned up the kitchen' and you're ready to start work.

Note that up until you light the incense you should carry out that part of the Ritual with closed eyes. Until you know it by heart, it is permissible to open your eyes whenever you need to read these instructions.

SECRET KEY III: RITUALS

Continue Now Call Your Cosmic Beings – They Await Your Commands

Now here's where Parts 3 through 9 of this Secret Key combine. The details of your Rituals are in those Parts. Under the title of the Ritual you'll find words and explanations, numbered 1 through 8. Those words and explanations fit right in here, as you call your Cosmic Beings to perform your Magic.

Having completed the Place-Cleaning Ritual, close your eyes and see the appropriate Arcane Admitting Password [Item 1 in the Ritual details] at the same time raising your hands in front of you just above eye level, and pretending to pull apart a set of drapes in front of you.

Announcing the Purpose of Your Call [Item 2 in the Ritual details]. Use the words given in the Ritual details, or use some of your own which mean the same thing. Say your Purpose three times, then tap 7 times with your knuckles on your altar.

Tell your Cosmic Being the names of the Planets you represent during the Ritual, by **naming them** aloud [Item 3 in the Ritual details].

Then say:

> "admit me....... [State the Name of the Cosmic Being who guards the Ritual you are working) and do my bidding as I command" [His name is Item 4 in the Ritual details.]

Knock on your altar seven times.

SECRET KEY III: RITUALS

Now **firmly state** what you wish to achieve [Item 5 in the Ritual details]. Use ordinary words, and make the statement as long or as short as you wish. Use the words in the Ritual details as an outline or guide, but you will find that your own thoughts and ways of stating your needs are more certain and more powerful.

Next, begin to quietly chant the Ritual's Avatar Mantrum [Item 6 in the Ritual details] in a slow rhythm, pronouncing it as written, with the same emphasis on each syllable. While you chant, with your eyes closed of course, pretend that your request has been granted: pretend that every last detail of the delights you have asked for have already arrived in a flood of power, light and happiness for you.

As you advance in your work, you may well see the form of the Cosmic Being you have called standing outside your Circle of Protection. This 'seeing' can either be a perfect, glowing confidence that a powerful and benevolent person is with you as you chant, or it can be a startling revelation of actually observing a Divine Form before you as you squint through your eyelashes to find out why the room has suddenly been flooded with light.

You can then be perfectly certain when that happens that your Ritual will be a resounding success in very short order.

Ending Your Ritual

Stop chanting the Avatar Mantrum after about five minutes, and then perform the following Dismissing Ritual.

SECRET KEY III: RITUALS

The Dismissing Ritual

As you stand before your altar, facing east, hands at your side, feet together.

Say:

> "I thank Thee, Cosmic Powers.
> "The Ritual is done.
> "All Forces, Entities and Energies
> "Shall go about their business
> "Until again I call.
> "In The Ultimate Name,
> "Go in peace to do my bidding.
> "So mote it be."

Bring your hands up in front of you and pretend to draw a set of drapes closed, just as you opened them near the start of the Ritual.

Close your eyes, if they are not already closed, and **Say**:

> "Fare thee well, all."

That expresses your gratitude to the Cosmic Beings and banishes the Elemental Powers which have been produced. It also ensures that any forces, harmless or otherwise, which have been attracted by the Ritual are ordered back to where they belong.

Magic Working is Simple and Automatic

That did not hurt a bit, did it? Naturally, the printed words here can give you a little idea of the stunning powers generated during your Ritual. Certainly, as you become more and more practiced, we will feel hot and cool flashes coursing throughout your body. And as previously suggested, you might actually see the Beings you are invoking for their friendliness and help.

All you need to do after your Magic Working is to put aside your Mystic Robe and Talisman, extinguish the candle and incense, coil up your Rope of Protection, and put things away until you wish to work at your next Magic.

If you wish, you can leave the Elemental Amulets and the Thaumaturgic Triplet in their places, but it is probably best to put them out of sight somewhere, so as not to excite the unnecessary interest of chance visitors to your Place of Working.

To build up the power, you can work any Ritual once a day. More often than that is undesirable. In fact, a good general rule of Magic is to concentrate on one Magical goal until it is successful and then move on to another.

By now you will no doubt have decided what miracles you wish to bring to pass in your life. Read the various Rituals in the following pages, and decide which one you will use first to bring happiness, power and wealth flowing to you. Then get to work, and may your every last dream appear in sparkling, glorious fulfilment as benevolent Cosmic Beings obey your commands.

SECRET KEY III: RITUALS

Part 3: Four Enriching Rituals to Produce All the Money and Luxury You Can Imagine

Each Ritual here is designed to be used in the Master Procedure which was given to you in Part 2. Names and how to say them, any special details, and the achievements each Ritual is designed for are handed to you in a way which simplifies Magic-Working to make it as easy as buttoning your coat. What a contrast with the complicated, confusing and deceptive grimoires which exist!

Apply the eight items of your chosen Ritual in the places indicated in the Master Procedure in Part 2, and you see your unsurpassed miracles happen. It's as simple as that!

The Rewarding Ticket-Come-To-Me Ritual

This Ritual has its most superlative effect if you work it a few days before you intend to buy a lottery ticket or to enter a competition where the prize depends purely on luck.

1. Arcane Admitting Password: ABALIM [pronounced "Ah-Bah-Limb," emphasis on final syllable].
2. The Purpose of Your Call: "My purpose is to win a prize in ...." [Name the lottery or competition you wish to win].
3. Planets Represented: Jupiter and Mercury.
4. Name of Cosmic Being: ATAPHIEL [pronounced "Ah-Tar-Fee-Ale," emphasis on second syllable]
5. What You Wish to Achieve: "I wish to win a large prize in the contest I have named. I will

SECRET KEY III: RITUALS

use the prize to benefit myself and my family by buying the luxuries we need."
6. Avatar Mantrum: ME-SAH-BOO
7. Best Time of Working: Monday, between 8 p.m. and 11 p.m., about one week after New Moon.
8. Mystic Talisman: No. 9

The Overwhelming Good-Luck-Is-Mine Ritual

This Ritual should be worked when things are going reasonably well for you, and you wish to increase your lucky breaks. If you are in a deep swing of misfortune and nothing is going right, the Genuine Bad-Luck-Banishing Ritual is the one to use.

1. Arcane Admitting Password: BARBATOS [pronounced "Bar-Bah-Toes," emphasis on first syllable].
2. The Purpose of Your Call: "My purpose is to seek aid in changing my luck to good.".
3. Planets Represented: Neptune and Jupiter
4. Name of Cosmic Being: BODIEL [pronounced "Bo-Dee-Ale," emphasis on second syllable].
5. What You Wish to Achieve: "I wish any bad luck I may have be banished forever. I ask for good fortune at all times." [State what kind of good fortune you are seeking].
6. Avatar Mantrum: BAY-ZAH-LEE-ALE
7. Best Time of Working: Tuesday, between sunset and dawn, about three days before Full Moon
8. Mystic Talisman: No. 1

SECRET KEY III: RITUALS

The Great Money-Spinning Ritual

If you wish to increase existing money, use this Ritual. Camaysar is a Genius who multiplies your existing assets, rather than creating something out of nothing. Compare the Miraculous Gold-Creating Ritual which follows this one.

1. Arcane Admitting Password: CORAEL [pronounced "Coe-Rah-Ale," emphasis on first syllable].
2. The Purpose of Your Call: "My purpose is to be helped to increase my personal assets."
3. Planets Represented: Mars and Jupiter.
4. Name of Cosmic Being: CAMAYSAR [pronounced "Car-May-Zar," emphasis on second syllable].
5. What You Wish to Achieve: "I wish to receive abundant cash which I shall use to pay off my debts, buy a home and enjoy an opulent life." [Be specific why you need money and what you will use it for].
6. Avatar Mantrum: CAR-RAH-CAR-SAW
7. Best Time of Working: Tuesday, any time, preferably just after New Moon.
8. Mystic Talisman: No. 8

The Miraculous Gold-Creating Ritual

Delukiel, the Cosmic Being you call to work this Ritual, is the One who can make money when you are in the depths of poverty. Decide if you need this Ritual, or the preceding Great Money-Spinning Ritual.

SECRET KEY III: RITUALS

1. Arcane Admitting Password: DARQUIEL [pronounced "Dar-Key-Ale," emphasis on the first syllable]
2. The Purpose of Your Call: "My purpose is to receive great wealth."
3. Planets Represented: Sun and Jupiter.
4. Name of Cosmic Being: DELUKIEL [pronounced "Day-Luke-Key-Ale," emphasis on second syllable].
5. What You Wish to Achieve: "I wish to be blessed with enough money and material wealth to last me for the rest of my days. I shall buy myself an island in the Bahamas and retire to a life of ease and enjoyment." [That's an example, of course. Specify exactly why you want money and how you will spend it].
6. Avatar Mantrum: DO-MA-REE-ALE
7. Best Time of Working: Friday, between 11 p.m. and midnight, at or near the Full Moon.
8. Mystic Talisman: No. 12

SECRET KEY III: RITUALS

Part 4: Three Power-Packed Rituals to Satisfy Your Lust and Love

The Titillating Nature Ritual

This Ritual is used to recreate physical abilities which have lessened or become weak due to illness or advancing age.

1. Arcane Admitting Password: EPITITIOKH [pronounced "Ape-Pea-Tea-Tea-Oak," emphasis on fourth syllable].
2. The Purpose of Your Call: "My purpose is to increase my physical powers."
3. Planets Represented: Mars and Sun.
4. Name of Cosmic Being: ELADEL [pronounced "Ale-Ah-Dale," emphasis on the final syllable].
5. What You Wish to Achieve: [use your own words to describe *exactly* what you wish to see happening to your physical self].
6. Avatar Mantrum: ABE-BOO-HOO-ALE
7. Best Time of Working: Saturday, any time after 4 p.m., a few days before Full Moon.
8. Mystic Talisman: No. 9

The Irresistible Bring-A-Lover Ritual

Furlac, this Ritual's Cosmic Being, will bring a lover to you suited to your current needs. If you are, for instance, sexually inhibited, expect either a partner who will stimulate you, or one who is not sexually demanding. As your tastes in lovers change, perform the Ritual again. A new lover, aligned with your requirements, will come to you *provided you have not married one of the previous ones in the meantime.* Marriage bonds are very powerful Magic, and if you

find yourself with a spouse, your best plan is to perform the Stimulating Partner-Enslaving Ritual which follows this one.

1. Arcane Admitting Password: FARUN FARO VAKSHUR [pronounced "Far-Run-Far-Oh-Vark-Sure," emphasis on fifth syllable.]
2. The Purpose of Your Call: "My purpose is to bring a lover to me."
3. Planets Represented: Venus and Pluto.
4. Name of Cosmic Being: FURLAC [rhymes with "Poor Jack"].
5. What You Wish to Achieve: "I wish to meet a lover who is exactly suited to my needs, who will be delighted with me and will satisfy my every desire."
6. Avatar Mantrum: FAR-VAR-DEEN
7. Best Time of Working: Wednesday, at 11 p.m., within three days of the Full Moon
8. Mystic Talisman: No. 8

The Stimulating Partner-Enslaving Ritual

This is primarily a love Ritual, but it can also be used with success in influencing the behaviour and decisions of a business partner.

1. Arcane Admitting Password: GUABAREL [pronounced "Goo-Ah-Bar-Ale," emphasis on the second syllable].
2. The Purpose of Your Call: "My purpose is to enslave a partner."
3. Planets Represented: Venus and Jupiter.
4. Name of Cosmic Being: GAMBIEL [pronounced "Gam-Bee-Ale," emphasis on final syllable].

SECRET KEY III: RITUALS

5. What You Wish to Achieve: "I wish to make........ [name the partner] a slave to my commands, obedient to my wishes, and willing to submit to all my requirements."
6. Avatar Mantrum: GAR-FEE-ALL.
7. Best Time of Working: Sunday, at any hour, at or just after New Moon.
8. Mystic Talisman: No. 5

Part 5: Three Miraculous Rituals to Restore Health and Bring Beauty and Potency to You.

Note:
These Rituals must not be used in the place of recognized and regular medical treatment. They should be used only in conjunction with your doctor's diagnoses, recommendations and prescriptions. Do not reveal to any medical person that you are performing the Rituals in this part, nor must you make any claims that Magic cured you when you return to health.

The Supreme Back-To-Health Ritual

The Ritual banishes general indispositions and brings glowing health and strength. If you have a specific disease, use the Secret Disease-Banishing Ritual which follows this one.

1. Arcane Admitting Password: IAOTH [pronounced "Ee-Ah-Oat," emphasis on the final syllable].
2. The Purpose of Your Call: "My purpose is to regain a healthy state."
3. Planets Represented: Saturn and Mercury.
4. Name of Cosmic Being: MUMIAH [pronounced "Moo-Me-Ah," emphasis on the first syllable].
5. What You Wish to Achieve: "I wish to regain my health and be free of............. [name the indispositions you wish to banish].
6. Avatar Mantrum: ISH-LEE-AH
7. Best Time of Working: Friday, during daylight hours *or* at 10 p.m., Moon waning from Full to New.
8. Mystic Talisman: No. 6

SECRET KEY III: RITUALS

The Secret Disease-Banishing Ritual

Find out the names of the diseases or maladies you are suffering from, and announce them to Heleleth. He will gladly reinforce the prescriptions and treatment recommended by your doctor.

1. Arcane Admitting Password: HARIEL [pronounced "Harry-Ale," emphasis on final syllable].
2. The Purpose of Your Call: "My purpose is to banish my disease."
3. Planets Represented: Mercury and Moon.
4. Name of Cosmic Being: HELELETH [pronounced "Hay-Lay-Late," emphasis on final syllable].
5. What You Wish to Achieve: "I wish to be cured of the following diseases:.......... [name your medical problems as precisely and accurately as you know them, including all symptoms]. I wish these diseases and their effects to be taken from me forever so that I may enjoy good health."
6. Avatar Mantrum: HEE-BALE-ZEE-WAH.
7. Best Time of Working: No special day or time.
8. Mystic Talisman: No. 4

The Fast Unwinding Ritual

This Ritual, although apparently minor in its application, is a fantastically powerful way of banishing physical tensions and nervousness. Miraculous transformations of self wellbeing are reported after working it.

SECRET KEY III: RITUALS

If possible, lie down flat on your bed for 30 minutes after performing the Ritual, quietly repeating the Avatar Mantrum.

During your day-to-day affairs, think the Avatar Mantrum whenever stress conditions occur. You will feel your tensions and nervousness draining away at once.

1. Arcane Admitting Password: JOSATA [pronounced "Yo-Sah-Tar," emphasis on second syllable].
2. The Purpose of Your Call: "My purpose is to physically relax."
3. Planets Represented: Uranus and Moon.
4. Name of Cosmic Being: JESUBILIN [pronounced "Yea-Sou-Bee-Lean," emphasis on second syllable].
5. What You Wish to Achieve: "I wish to be relieved of all tensions and their negative results so that I may be relaxed, harmonious and free."
6. Avatar Mantrum: YAY-DO-TUN
7. Best Time of Working: Monday, at any hour, but almost equally effective on any day.
8. Mystic Talisman: No. 3

SECRET KEY III: RITUALS

Part 6: Three Crushing Rituals to Give You Supreme Power over Others

The Explosive Eye-Glance Ritual

This Ritual produces an inner power which radiates from your eyes. When speaking to anyone, look between his or her eyes at the bridge of the nose. However, make this glance only occasionally: as with all Magic, you must not attract attention to its use. Do not try to 'stare down' the person you are influencing.

Used in conjunction with hypnotic techniques, this Ritual amplifies hypnotic powers by an infinite amount.

1. Arcane Admitting Password: KATZFIEL [pronounced "Cats-Fee-Ale," emphasis on first syllable].
2. The Purpose of Your Call: "My purpose is to overwhelm others with my glance."
3. Planets Represented: Moon and Sun.
4. Name of Cosmic Being: KEVEQEL [pronounced "Kay-Vay-Kale," emphasis on second syllable].
5. What You Wish to Achieve: "I wish to gain a powerful personality which will over-come the wills of others by means of a level gaze. When I acquire this ability I will use it to ...."[Name your purpose; Keveqel will be interested to know].
6. Avatar Mantrum: KAFF-KAFF-EE-ALE
7. Best Time of Working: Most powerful on the day of Full Moon, but effective at all times.
8. Mystic Talisman: No. 7

SECRET KEY III: RITUALS

The Magical Win-In-Battle Ritual

Think of this Ritual as a means of overcoming all oppositions in life. Use it before being confronted by anyone with whom you need to reach an agreement or before you enter any kind of competitive situation.

1. Arcane Admitting Password: LOQUEL [pronounced "Low-Kale," emphasis on first syllable].
2. The Purpose of Your Call: "My purpose is to be victorious in all I attempt."
3. Planets Represented: Mars and Saturn.
4. Name of Cosmic Being: LIBABRIS [pronounced "Lee-Bah-Breeze," emphasis on second syllable].
5. What You Wish to Achieve: "I wish to acquire the power to win the coming contest, when I shall be in conflict with ...." [state who or what you will be battling against and what you will do when you have won].
6. Avatar Mantrum: LA-MA
7. Best Time of Working: Wednesday, midnight, near New Moon.
8. Mystic Talisman: No. 1

The Volcanic You-Will-Submit Ritual

Use this Ritual to make a particular person obey your wishes. If the situation requires you to overcome several people, or you're not sure to whom you will be opposed, use the Explosive Eye-Glance Ritual or the Magical Win-In-Battle Ritual.

SECRET KEY III: RITUALS

1. Arcane Admitting Password: MEHUMAN [pronounced "May-Hoo-Man, emphasis on second syllable].
2. The Purpose of Your Call: "My purpose is to impose my will on others."
3. Planets Represented: Neptune and Pluto.
4. Name of Cosmic Being: MELHA [pronounced "Male-Ha," emphasis on last syllable].
5. What You Wish to Achieve: "I wish to overcome............" [name the person or condition you wish to overcome and then state what actions you will take after you have achieved the submission].
6. Avatar Mantrum: MAY-MOON-EYE
7. Best Time of Working: Saturday, between sunset and midnight, close to Full Moon.
8. Mystic Talisman: No. 11

SECRET KEY III: RITUALS

Part 7: Three Stupendous Rituals to Transform Your Personal Relationships

The Titanic Enemies-Vanquished Ritual

Before you work this Ritual, you must be absolutely sure that you have enemies. If you are merely in a cycle of ill luck, and only suspect that others are causing your troubles, then use the Genuine Bad-Luck-Banishing Ritual.

1. Arcane Admitting Password: NURIEL [pronounced "Noo-Ree-Ale," emphasis on second syllable].
2. The Purpose of Your Call: "My purpose is to vanquish my enemies."
3. Planets Represented: Uranus and Venus.
4. Name of Cosmic Being: NARUDI [pronounced "Nah-Rue-Dee," emphasis on last syllable].
5. What You Wish to Achieve: "I wish to be victorious over.........." [state who or what you wish to vanquish, then say what you will do when victory is yours.
6. Avatar Mantrum: NAY-REE-ALE.
7. Best Time of Working: Tuesday, noon or midnight, close to Full Moon.
8. Mystic Talisman: No. 10

The Astounding Change-Opinions-Of-Others Ritual

Carefully review your main goal in life before working this Ritual. Onafiel works most efficiently when He can focus on a particular target for you.

SECRET KEY III: RITUALS

1. Arcane Admitting Password: OCTINOMON [pronounced "Oak-Tea-No-Moan," emphasis on second syllable].
2. The Purpose of Your Call: "My purpose is to influence the opinion of others."
3. Planets Represented: Neptune and Moon.
4. Name of Cosmic Being: ONAFIEL [pronounced "Own-Ah-Fee-Ale," emphasis on second syllable].
5. What You Wish to Achieve: "I wish to achieve the ability to change the thoughts of others to my advantage. When I have this talent I will use it to............." [say exactly what you intend to do with this ability].
6. Avatar Mantrum: OH-ROE-MA-SEEM
7. Best Time of Working: Thursday, 10 p.m. to 11 p.m. three days after New Moon.
8. Mystic Talisman: No. 2

The Power Take-Me-To-The-Top Ritual

Decide exactly what you wish to become in what field. The more precise your commands, the more accurately Umeroz can execute them.

1. Arcane Admitting Password: UZIPHIEL [pronounced "Ooze-Ee-Fee-Ale," emphasis on second syllable].
2. The Purpose of Your Call: "My purpose is to rise to the top of my chosen field."
3. Planets Represented: Uranus and Pluto.
4. Name of Cosmic Being: UMEROZ [pronounced "Oo-May-Rose," emphasis on first syllable].
5. What You Wish to Achieve: "I wish to reach the pinnacle of success as............." [say what you wish to become].

SECRET KEY III: RITUALS

6. Avatar Mantrum: OO-VAH-YAH
7. Best Time of Working: Monday, after sunset, within seven days of New Moon.
8. Mystic Talisman: No. 12

SECRET KEY III: RITUALS

Part 8: Five Amazing Rituals for Success in Your Job, Career and Business.

The Forceful Buy-Sell Ritual

If you can specify what product, item or service you wish to deal in, your chances for success are considerably enhanced. This Ritual is very much orientated toward trade and business.

1. Arcane Admitting Password: QUELAMIA [pronounced "Kay-Lamb-Me-Yah," emphasis on third syllable].
2. The Purpose of Your Call: "My purpose is to achieve success in my dealings."
3. Planets Represented: Uranus and Saturn.
4. Name of Cosmic Being: QANIEL [pronounced "Car-Knee-Ale," emphasis on second syllable].
5. What You Wish to Achieve: "I wish to become powerful in buying and selling. My chief reason for wishing to acquire this power is to............" [state your reason, and announce what you will do with your life when the power is yours. Qaniel has a fatherly interest in those he assists].
6. Avatar Mantrum: KAFF-SEE-ALE.
7. Best Time of Working: Friday, any time.
8. Mystic Talisman: No. 4

The Automatic Test-Success Ritual

As you will note under Item 5 of this Ritual, be prepared beforehand to describe the test and its details clearly to Ram Avatar. As with all Magic, precision of aim brings greater success than general or "scatter-gun" requests.

SECRET KEY III: RITUALS

1. Arcane Admitting Password: REMPHA [rhymes with "Came far"].
2. The Purpose of Your Call: "My purpose is to pass a test successfully."
3. Planets Represented: Moon and Pluto.
4. Name of Cosmic Being: RAM AVATAR [pronounced "Rahm-Ah-Vah-Tar," emphasis on third syllable].
5. What You Wish to Achieve: "I wish to be supremely successful in the future test which will take place................" [Name the time, date, place and subject of the test, then say why you need to pass and what you will gain from it.]
6. Avatar Mantrum: RAH-HA-BEE-ALE.
7. Best Time of Working: No particular time.
8. Mystic Talisman: No. 3

The Delightful Tell-Me-My-Powers Ritual

You have talents which are as yet undiscovered or not yet fully used. After working this Ritual, relax in a chair and let your mind flow freely. Listen to any impulses or hunches on what project or subject it might be useful for you to pursue.

Thereafter, promptly accept all chances which come your way to improve your existing skills, or to try your hand at new occupations, hobbies or crafts.

1. Arcane Admitting Password: SANGARIEL [pronounced "Sang-Are-Ree-Ale," emphasis on second syllable].
2. The Purpose of Your Call: "My purpose is to learn my inner powers and talents."
3. Planets Represented: Sun and Venus.

SECRET KEY III: RITUALS

    4. Name of Cosmic Being: SHATHNIEL [pronounced "Shat-Knee-Ale," emphasis on first syllable].
    5. What You Wish to Achieve: "I wish to know what my inner powers are, to enable me to find greater success, freedom and harmony in the world.
    6. Avatar Mantrum: SAM-HE-ALE.
    7. Best Time of Working: Sunday, early morning or late evening, close to Full Moon.
    8. Mystic Talisman: No. 9

The Thrilling I-Can-Wow-Them Ritual

Use this Ritual before you make a personal appearance in front of an audience. This applies to lectures, appeals, addresses and presentations as well as show business work.

    1. Arcane Admitting Password: TIKARATHIN [pronounced "Tea-Car-Are-Teen," emphasis on last syllable].
    2. The Purpose of Your Call: "My purpose is to be able to project my personality."
    3. Planets Represented: Pluto and Sun.
    4. Name of Cosmic Being: TORQUARET [pronounced "Talk-Are-Ate," emphasis on last syllable].
    5. What You Wish to Achieve: "I wish to achieve acclaim and applause from audiences. In particular, I wish to be a special success………………" [name the occasion, the time, date and place. Then say what prime ambition you expect to achieve].
    6. Avatar Mantrum: TOUR-ME-ALE.
    7. Best Time of Working: Saturday, at any hour.

8. Mystic Talisman: No. 6

The Unique Know-What-Comes Ritual

Knowing the future gives you tremendous advantages. If you are prompted to learn any fortune-telling techniques, such as card reading, palm reading, crystal ball gazing or other psychic pursuits, do not hesitate to master the art: that will be Vocasiel offering you the clearest way to see the future.

After working the Ritual, listen for and obey all hunches and intuitions which reach you, and note what information about the future is given to you in your dreams.

1. Arcane Admitting Password: VARUNA [pronounced "Vah-Rune-Are," emphasis on last syllable].
2. The Purpose of Your Call: "My purpose is to foresee the future."
3. Planets Represented: Saturn and Jupiter.
4. Name of Cosmic Being: VOCASIEL [pronounced "Voke-Car-Sea-Ale," emphasis on second syllable].
5. What You Wish to Achieve: "I wish to have the doors of time opened for me, so that I may see the future. I shall use this ability................." [say why you need this power, and what is the first major use you will make of it].
6. Avatar Mantrum: VO-WHO-MA-NAH.
7. Best Time of Working: Wednesday, after dark, Moon between New and Full, i.e. waxing.
8. Mystic Talisman: No. 1

SECRET KEY III: RITUALS

Part 9: Six Ultimately Powerful Rituals to Bring Superlative Benefits to You.

The Marvelous See-Where Ritual

Use this Ritual to find lost objects. Describe the missing item clearly to Weatta, and after the Ritual, sit in a darkened room and pay attention to your stream of thoughts, and anything else going on in your head. Write down and act on the information received.

1. Arcane Admitting Password: WALLIM [pronounced "Wall-Eem," emphasis on second syllable].
2. The Purpose of Your Call: "My purpose is to find that which is lost."
3. Planets Represented: Moon and Venus.
4. Name of Cosmic Being: WEATTA [pronounced "Way-Ah-Tar," emphasis on second syllable].
5. What You Wish to Achieve: "I wish to be granted the power of knowing the exact whereabouts of............ " [state what you are seeking, and where it was last seen].
6. Avatar Mantrum: OH-MOE-FOR-US.
7. Best Time of Working: Wednesday, after dark, Moon waxing from New to Full.
8. Mystic Talisman: No. 10

The Ideal Change-My-Home Ritual

Best results are achieved when you know where you wish to go. However, if you have no new home in mind, Purah will locate one for you. Naturally, you will deal with the physical arrangements for moving your belongings. Also remember you are seeking happiness in your new abode: its physical dimensions may not measure up to what you were expecting; Purah, however, is aware of the future and may decide that you will find happiness in a small apartment and only misery in a mansion.

1. Arcane Admitting Password: PHATIAL [pronounced "Far-Tea-Ale," emphasis on first syllable].
2. The Purpose of Your Call: "My purpose is to move to a different home."
3. Planets Represented: Mercury and Mars.
4. Name of Cosmic Being: PURAH [Pronounced "Poor-Ah," emphasis on second syllable].
5. What You Wish to Achieve: "I wish to leave my present abode and find happiness in another one." [If you have a new home already in mind, say so, giving the address].
6. Avatar Mantrum: POO-ROO-SHAH.
7. Best Time of Working: Sunday, 9 p.m. to 11 p.m. or during daylight, close to New Moon.
8. Mystic Talisman: No. 8

The Flashing Cause-Discord Ritual

People must be deliberately harming or maliciously opposing you before you lay the devastating Powers of Xomoy on them.

1. Arcane Admitting Password: XATHANAEL [pronounced "Zat-Ann-Ah-Yale," emphasis on second syllable].
2. The Purpose of Your Call: "My purpose is to cause discord among my enemies."
3. Planets Represented: Mars and Venus.

SECRET KEY III: RITUALS

4. Name of Cosmic Being: XOMOY [pronounced "Zomoy" and rhymes with "Oh, boy!"].
5. What You Wish to Achieve: "I wish to see turmoil break out between............." [name those you wish to see disrupted].
6. Avatar Mantrum: ZONE-OR.
7. Best Time of Working: Tuesday, any hour.
8. Mystic Talisman: No. 5

The Arcane Invisibility Ritual

Tread carefully with this Ritual. It's very ancient and has ramifications which a beginner might not consider.

The best way to operate initially is to complete the Ritual and then sit quietly in a chair. Close your eyes and pretend that you are in a place where you wish to discover secrets. As you make progress in cooperation with Yeshayah, you will find you are carried, in your mind, to your destination, where you may clearly know what is going on.

This, in fact, is better than physical invisibility: even when you have become invisible to others, you will still be unable to pass through locked doors or to enter a room without opening the door. Physical invisibility is really a cloak of influence which surrounds you, so that, although you are actually there, the people present do not see you. Yet they will see doors opening and closing as you go in and out, and if someone walks into you, you will both feel the impact, even though the person will not know what he has walked into.

True invisibility comes when you have total faith and familiarity in Yeshayah, and have met Him by your altar several times. He will tell you when you are ready to actually walk invisibly in the streets, or sit unseen in a room.

Be especially careful crossing roads when you are invisible: the drivers cannot see you, but the vehicles will hit you just as hard as they would in your normal state.

1. Arcane Admitting Password: YEBEMEL [pronounced "Yay-Bay-Male," emphasis on second syllable].
2. The Purpose of Your Call: "My purpose is to travel invisibly to discover secrets".
3. Planets Represented: Uranus and Neptune
4. Name of Cosmic Being: YESHAYAH [pronounced "Yah-Shah-Yah," emphasis on second syllable].
5. What You Wish to Achieve: "I wish to move unseen, taking my eyes and ears invisibly to............." [state where you wish to go and what you intend to do while you are invisible].
6. Avatar Mantrum: YAH-HA-LA.
7. Best Time of Working: Friday, between 6 p.m. and midnight, New Moon or thereabouts.
8. Mystic Talisman: No. 11

The Great Bad-Luck-Banishing Ritual

Work this Ritual when your life is at its worst. Zeffar gladly accepts the challenge of banishing misery caused by heavy ill-luck vibrations.

SECRET KEY III: RITUALS

He is less keen on changing your life if you are merely seeking to improve your luck. Instead, use the Overwhelming Good-Luck-Is-Mine Ritual. And if misfortunes are being caused by hexing or Black Magic, use Titanic Enemies-Vanquished Ritual.

1. Arcane Admitting Password: ZEBURIAL [pronounced "Zay-Boor-Ee-Ale," emphasis on second syllable].
2. The Purpose of Your Call: "My purpose is to banish my bad luck."
3. Planets Represented: Jupiter and Moon.
4. Name of Cosmic Being: ZEFFAR [pronounced "Zay-Far," emphasis on second syllable].
5. What You Wish to Achieve: "I wish to totally banish my bad luck and replace it with harmony and happiness. In particular, I wish to banish ...." [say exactly what influences you wish to have taken away].
6. Avatar Mantrum: ZOO-RAY-ALE.
7. Best Time of Working: Thursday, any hour.
8. Mystic Talisman: No. 2

The Mysterious Enemy-Repulsion Ritual

Turmiel is adept at turning away the turmoil caused by enemies. You should be able to name them, and be sure they are actually attacking you. This Ritual will protect you from their negative actions. If you wish to hurt them, use the Titanic Enemies-Vanquished Ritual.

1. Arcane Admitting Password: TISHBASH [pronounced as spelled].
2. The Purpose of Your Call: "My purpose is to hurl my enemies from me."

SECRET KEY III: RITUALS

3. Planets Represented: Mars and Neptune.
4. Name of Cosmic Being: TURMIEL [pronounced "Tour-Me-Ale," emphasis on first syllable].
5. What You Wish to Achieve: "I wish to protect myself from................" [name your enemy or enemies] and send confusion and pain."
6. Avatar Mantrum: TAR-SHE-SHEEM.
7. Best Time of Working: Saturday, midnight, at New Moon.
8. Mystic Talisman: No. 7

Secret Key IV: CAPITALIZING ON MAGIC

Your Personal Program of Magic-Working to Produce Your Wonderful Horn of Plenty

The details of secret Magic Working which have been presented to you are based on years of careful research. You now have all you need so that you too can bring perfection to every aspect of your life – easily, accurately and automatically.

Such a feast of Magic has maybe left you wondering where to begin. So follow the suggestions in this Secret Key, and make yourself over into rich, harmonious, happy, powerful and satisfied being.

Decide on the Miracle You Need First

Sit back for a moment. What is it right now which worries, frustrates or aggravates you the most? Lack of money? An unsatisfying relationship? Your own ill-health? Your general bad luck? An irritating enemy? Some or all of those, or something else?

You will find that your best course by far is to first get rid of whatever you find yourself dwelling on when you are down. Once you have identified your problem, flick through these pages until you find the Spell or Ritual you need.

Here somewhere is the Magic which can easily dispose of that worry or irritation. Apply that Magic, and see your major problem vanish into limbo.

SECRET KEY IV: CAPITALIZING ON MAGIC

Next, Dispose of Minor Irritations Which Prevent You Enjoying Life to the Full

Obviously, if you are suffering from the opinions of others, or you find some other negative factor is holding you back from enjoying life, you need to alter that condition before proceeding further. You understand that even a roomful of gold coins will not be enough to bring you total happiness if there are other aspects of your life which need changing.

Feelings of self-confidence, the sparkle of a bright intelligent mind and the surge and spring of a youthful body are just as important as surplus cash.

So work some of these incredible Spells and Rituals to bring yourself health, virility, quickness of brain and attractiveness. Vanquish your enemies with a quick blast of Magic.

Then move in on bringing cash flooding to you in a golden shower which will make an oil magnate green with envy.

That's probably one of the most important thoughts in these pages: acquire health, self-assurance, good luck, and then add money to make your life perfect, satisfying and fulfilling.

When You are Ready for it, Make Money by the Truckload

Think about the details before you work your Magic. If you are calling up a luxurious car with stereo, bar and telephone, do you have somewhere to keep it?

Maybe you'd better get yourself a new ranch style home on its own parkland first.

All planned? All ready to let Magic take you to that peak of the mountain of money, satisfaction and ecstasy you're yearning for? So what are you waiting for? Take the Spell and Ritual you fancy and go for it!

Do What Thou Will, If It Harm None

You're all set now. Think how your life is about to be transformed, with the help of Cosmic Beings who are waiting to serve you, who know what you need almost before you ask. Nothing can stand in your way.

So move on up the ladder to wealth, health, supreme happiness, power, love and success, using the magnificent Powers of Magic.

I've given you the key: open the door and take what you desire.

So mote it be..

Secret Key V:
ONE SPELL BY VcToria

One Spell by VcToria

VcToria has decided to add one Spell here at the end of her late Father's book. Before I do, please know that Dad was felt in every energy way possible as I typed his book in. His favorite numbers were 222. While he lived in British Columbia, Canada he made sure to have his license plate on his vehicle be 222. Every day that I worked on this book and looked up at my clock it read 222 in some form.

Although he published the book under Frater Malak his real name was Geof Gray-Cobb. He spelt Geof without the extra F. This also led to the name adding to a 6. His Life Path number was 16/7. Mine is too.

I have carried on his work with requests from those who enjoyed his work. He had many fans and I wish that the internet had been here in his time, in his youth, while he was creating Magic. I believe he will return to this life time at some point and continue his work in different avenues.

Each time you buy a Talisman and Amulet Kit I channel his energy and ask that the supreme Magic energy that he implanted into them with his books be the same for those who request them.

Within this book I also request that the energy he intended to implant to you all, be stronger now that I have joined forces with it.

Here is a Spell I have channelled from him, and with his permission from the other side added it to the book. It is also the time where I take the Talisman and Amulet Kits and impress into them the same

SECRET KEY V: ONE SPELL BY VCTORIA

energy that my Father did. **This is why they are sent out separately from the book.**

The Moon must be present in Pisces. In my monthly newsletter that you may sign up for, I give the Moon placements. Once or twice a month the Moon will be in Pisces.

1. Time: Moon must be in Pisces. Use any hour.
2. Location: A room with silence. You may also do this while traveling, in your hotel room.
3. Essential Oil: Lavender or Patchouli.
4. Candle: White.
5. Incense: Patchouli or any scent that brings you relaxation.

Instructions: We will be using my late Father to channel all your requests to the correct guide that deals with requests from Magic.

Sit in the room with the candle lit. You may use your altar for this, or your special place. Light your incense on your altar or special place. Take your essential oil and drop a few drops on your left hand, on the forefinger. Dab your forehead 11 times. Each time you dab, say the name Geof or Frater. Say this name slowly and intently, keeping in mind that you are calling a Being from the other side. If you can visualize what Geof/Frater looked like then all the better.

You have now called in the power of Geof Gray Cobb by using that name or Frater Malak.

Feel the silence and the shift in energy. Lie or sit, whatever is comfortable. Now ask that your spiritual world come to you along with your own guides and put in the protection request. "I request that my guides protect me from any outside forces that are uninvited".

Once having done that, speak to Geof or Frater, whoever you have chosen to call my Dad. Ask him to 'relay your request……….. ["say what it is"] and then ask that he take it to the correct source, who will then send the answer to you'.

Lie quietly for 15 to 30 minutes, envisioning that whatever you asked for be done. Once you have decided that your time is up, please, before you stir, **say:**

> "All who have been here to help, you may leave and return the next time I call with the Pisces Moon."

Then say:

> "Thank you Universe for all You do For Me."

Then end it with saying:

> "May Peace be granted for you, The Universe, and may you share that Peace with me."

Get up, bow to the East if it is day, and West if it is night time. Remember it is a once or twice a month only opportunity, so set your cell phones to remind you.

This spell is 'POWER' from beyond and adjoined with Power from myself. Know that I am always aware

SECRET KEY V: ONE SPELL BY VCTORIA

when the Moon is in Pisces and do my own meditations at that time. I will, from this day forth, include all of the people who have been good enough to still maintain my Fathers work, in my sending of energy. In other words, I will be helping anyone who is administrating the Spell during this time frame.

As my Father always uses "So Mote It be," I use:

Positive Thoughts to You All

Frater Malak